KENNETH G. RAINIS

ENVIRONMENTAL SCIENCE PROJECTS FOR YOUNG SCIENTISTS

FRANKLIN WATTS
NEW YORK | CHICAGO | LONDON | TORONTO | SYDNEY

Photographs copyright © Bruce J. Russell, BioMEDIA Associates, Loomis, Ca., and the author

Library of Congress Cataloging-in-Publication Data

Rainis, Kenneth G.
    Environmental projects for young scientists / Kenneth G. Rainis.
        p.   cm.
    Includes bibliographical references and index.
    ISBN 0-531-11194-6 (lib. bdg.)
    1. Environmental sciences—Study and teaching—Activity programs—
Juvenile literature.   [1. Environmental sciences—Experiments.
    2. Experiments.]   I. Title.
    GE77.R35   1994
    363.7'0078-dc20   94-26876
                                                               CIP AC

FOR MY MOTHER, ANN RAINIS,
WHOSE LOVE, ENCOURAGEMENT, AND
SUPPORT HELPED SHOW ME
THE WAY

ACKNOWLEDGMENTS

This book could not have become a reality without the support and encouragement of my wife, Joan, and my children, Michael and Caroline.

Tom Cohn, my original editor, suggested writing this book, and gave me the freedom to explore and develop the ideas presented here. Karen Fitzgerald helped me polish the rough edges and has been a source of encouragement and feedback.

The individuals whose critiques helped make this a more accessible work for young scientists are Peg Schoenfield, master teacher at Jefferson Avenue School in Fairport, New York, whose enthusiastic support throughout my writing years helped keep me on the right track; my friends and colleagues George Nassis and Robert Iveson, who also reviewed the manuscript with a critical eye toward "making sure it's fun"!

John Elberfeld contributed his vast expertise in things digital, helping digitize the illustrations presented here. My son, Michael, a budding young artist, also assisted in certain illustrations, making sure I got the perspective right!

Special thanks go to Bruce Russell of Bio-MEDIA Associates, for his detailed critique as well as his many photographs, including the cover, which help open up the natural world to young readers.

CONTENTS

CHAPTER 1
What Is Your Environment Like?
11

CHAPTER 2
Biodiversity: The Spice of Life!
19

CHAPTER 3
Recycling: Nature's Way and Otherwise!
43

CHAPTER 4
Living Water
75

CHAPTER 5
The Land
103

CHAPTER 6
The Air We All
Breathe!
121

CHAPTER 7
Ten Projects to Help
the Environment
142

Appendix
Where to Obtain
Materials
154

Index
156

ENVIRONMENTAL SCIENCE
PROJECTS FOR YOUNG SCIENTISTS

1

WHAT IS YOUR ENVIRONMENT LIKE?

THE PROJECTS IN THIS BOOK

The projects in this book are designed to help you learn more about the environment the—natural world about you—as well as how we affect it. Some of the projects are easy; some are difficult. Some are presented in step-by-step fashion, like a laboratory investigation, while others are simply ideas for you to develop.

You can walk through the projects systematically to learn more about both the biological and the physical aspects of our environment, or you can choose one project that appeals to you. Either way, you will wind up with an experience that is enriching for its own sake, that may satisfy a class requirement, or that may be suitable for a science fair project.

Be sure to refer to the Learn More About It and Read More About It sections at the end of every chapter. They contain a wealth of information concerning where to go to locate study materials or obtain additional information about a chapter topic.

Since classroom assignments and science fairs require careful methodology and formal presentation, you may need to do much planning before you actually begin a project, and you will want to take careful notes in your field notebook as you go along. For example, even though your project may consist of probing the inner-space world of soil particles in studying how pesticides affect microlife populations, you will want to organize your findings in a coherent fashion so that it doesn't appear that all you have done is to make some random observations with your microscope.

Throughout your work, use an orderly process of inquiry, beginning with an *observation*:

$$\text{OBSERVE} \rightarrow \text{GUESS} \rightarrow \text{TEST} \rightarrow \text{CONCLUDE}$$

Observe carefully, keeping accurate records of what is happening around you; make a *guess* (a hypothesis) to explain what you have observed; design a method (an experiment) to *test* your guess; and use your results (data) to *conclude* whether your guess was correct or whether it should be changed. Sometimes you will need to establish a *control group* against which to compare your results. A control group helps you determine whether your experimental results are valid.

Your powers of observation will provide the springboard for your investigations. At times, your investigations will be aided by serendipity—the art of finding something valuable when you are looking for something else. As the great scientist Louis Pasteur said, "Chance favors the prepared mind."

WHAT'S YOUR BIOME?

Biomes are areas with characteristic plant types. In North America, there are twelve major biomes: tundra, taiga, coniferous forest, coniferous forest-grassland, coniferous forest-hardwood, deciduous forest, southern pine-deciduous, grassland, sagebrush, desert, chaparral, and rain forest. See Figure 1-1. Human intervention or a natural disaster (insect infestation, fire, hurricane, flood, and so on) can remove the stable and sustaining vegetation called *climax vegetation*, but over time it will reappear if the region is left undisturbed. This restoration process is called *succession*.

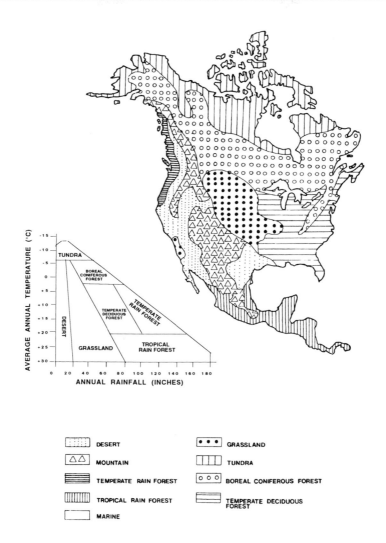

Figure 1-1   North American Biomes

• Identify the biome you live in, or others nearby. Locate a healthy *community*—a place, such as a pond or a log, where several populations of organisms live—within the biome. Pick a place that is minimally affected by human activity.

• In your field notebook, make a list of all the *biotic* components (living things) you observe within the community and group them by kingdom. (There are five recognized kingdoms: Bacteria, Fungi, Protists, Plants, and Animals; see chapter 2.) For each identified organism, determine its *trophic level* (what each organism eats): is it a *producer* (a green plant that makes its own food), a *consumer* (an animal that feeds on producers or other consumers), or a *decomposer* (an organism that feeds on animal wastes or dead matter)?

• Construct *food chains* for your community—pathways for the recycling of nutrients through producers, consumers, and decomposers back to producer. The sum of all of these interconnecting networks of food chains is a *food web*—a graphic picture of how energy and materials move through a community.

• Take careful notes concerning physical (*abiotic*) factors: amounts of sunlight and shade, average temperature and temperature range, type of soil (see chapter 5), and average precipitation (see chapter 4). Look at their distribution within the community you are studying. Compare your climatic data with data presented in Figure 1-1. Does the presence of a mountain range or a large body of water (lake or ocean) affect the community or biome? Can you draw any conclusions concerning how abiotic and biotic factors affect the community?

• If possible, study adjacent biomes when you take a trip. Do biomes fade into each other, or is there a sharp break between them?

DESIGNING A BIOSPHERE

In several places in the United States and in other countries, scientists are designing and testing environments called *closed ecosystems* to help them understand the problems that must be overcome if humans are ever to live for an extended time on the moon or on one of the planets.

In a closed ecosystem, no molecules can enter or leave; everything is recycled: water, gases, nutrients, waste products, and life-forms.

Some designs are already in use. Many popular magazine articles have been written about the ongoing *Biosphere II* project (the earth is Biosphere I) in Oracle, Arizona. Beginning in 1991, a team of eight men and women ("biosphereans") spent two years living within a 3.15-acre (1.3 ha) enclosed glass-and-steel dome housing five biomes. They produced their own food while recycling air, water, and waste in a prototype space colony. They strove for self-sufficiency, though they did not quite attain it.

Although you will not be able to seal in *every* molecule, you can experiment with closed ecosystems. They can be as large or as small as you want. To get started, use several large, wide-mouthed glass jars to enclose your aquatic ecosystems. The long-term success of your systems will depend upon which life-forms you select. For any system to work properly (remain balanced), you may have to use trial and error to obtain the right balance of producers, consumers, and decomposers.

To construct a closed ecosystem, add washed aquarium gravel (or field-collected pea-gravel from a stream) to a mason jar to a depth of about 1 inch (2.5 cm). Slowly add pond water (or aged tap or bottled distilled water) to fill the jar halfway. Plant rooted aquatic plants (*Elodea, Sagittaria,* moneywort—available at aquarium stores) in the gravel. Let water clear for a day or two. Next, add scavengers (mystery snail—*Ampullaria,* or small fingernail clam) and consumers (one or two fish such as neon tetras or guppies). Try varying the "consumer ratio"—the number of consumers (low) to producers (high)—in each of several "trial ecosystems." Add more water to fill the jar to within 2 inches (5 cm) of the top. Use clear plastic wrap (seal tightly using rubber bands) to provide a temporary seal.

Place your trial systems in a location having a stable temperature (around 68°F[20°C]) and receiving 16 hours per day of either indirect natural (north light) or artificial light (place a 60- or 75-watt incandescent bulb about 8 inches (20 cm) from the top of the jar.)

Once you seal and position your system, watch it carefully. For example, the water may turn very green, signaling an imbalance. You may have to adjust the height of the light source or use a lower wattage bulb, or perhaps remove or add a scavenger or consumer, or replace a volume of water. You may even have to start over!

When you think that a particular miniature ecosystem has achieved balance (wait at least 1 month), replace the temporary plastic wrap cover with a piece of glass plate (cut to match the dimensions of the jar opening); seal with aquarium cement.

Use the chapters of this book and the other resources in Read More About It to learn more about the various biogeochemical cycles that work in harmony to cycle nutrients within your miniature ecosystem.

SAFETY—THE MOST IMPORTANT PART OF ANY PROJECT

Eleven rules to keep safe:

1. Be serious about science. A careless attitude can be dangerous to you and to others.

2. *Never* look into a lens (or other optical instrument) pointed directly at the sun or capturing direct sun rays. Doing so can cause serious injury to your eyes.

3. Read instructions carefully before starting any project outlined in this book. If you plan to expand on these activities, discuss your experimental procedure with a science teacher or a knowledgeable adult before going ahead.

4. Keep your work area clean and organized. Never eat or drink while conducting experiments.

5. Respect all life-forms. Never mishandle organisms or perform an experiment that will injure or harm them.

6. Wear protective personal equipment—eye goggles, protective gloves, and a smock or apron—when doing projects involving chemicals, when heating objects or water, or when performing any other experiment that could lead to eye injury.

7. Do not touch chemicals with your bare hands. Do not taste chemicals or chemical solutions. Avoid inhaling vapors or fumes of any chemical or chemical solution.

8. Clean up any chemical spill immediately. If you spill anything on your skin or clothing, rinse it off immediately with plenty of water. Then report what happened to a responsible adult.

9. Keep flammable and combustible materials away from heat sources and sparks.

10. *Never* operate a power tool without direct adult supervision.

11. *Always* wash your hands after conducting activities. Dispose of contaminated waste or articles properly.

Learn More About It

ENVIRONMENTAL ELECTRONIC DATABASE

Free on-line computer link to help you find information and share ideas about specific environmental issues. Contact *EarthNet:* 50 Udalia Road, West Islip, NY 11795. Phone (516)669-0138. Connect through (516)321-4893.

Read More About It

Margulis, Lynn, and Karlene Schwartz. *Five Kingdoms: An Illustrated Guide to the Phyla of Life on Earth.* 2nd ed. New York: Freeman, 1988.

Rainis, Kenneth. *Nature Projects for Young Scientists*. New York: Watts, 1989.

Sagan, Carl. *Cosmos*. New York: Random House, 1980.

Taub, F. B. "Closed Ecosystems." *Annual Review of Ecology and Systematics*. 5:139-160, 1974.

2

BIODIVERSITY:
THE SPICE OF LIFE!

All life-forms on earth are dependent upon one another. The interplay between organisms and their environment makes possible the diversity of life that exists today.

The living planet is a system in balance maintained through the interaction of organisms—big, small, or invisible to our eyes— each acting as a producer, consumer, or decomposer.

Species diversity is the window by which environmental biologists assess the health of an ecosystem: habitats that enjoy large numbers of different species are more healthy than those that have large numbers of a few species. Within any given habitat the greatest diversity revolves around small organisms, mostly because of their size and almost boundless numbers within a biological community.

The primary cause of species diversity reduction is habitat destruction. Man's activities threaten the Earth's diversity and balance in ways that are immediately recognizable and insidious: clear-cutting of tropical rain forests (over 28 million acres), increased desertification through overgrazing, and acid deposition, are slowly destroying whole forest ecosystems and adding over 19 billion tons of carbon dioxide to the atmosphere, thus aggravating the global warming process.

For advanced young scientists

COMMUNITY MEETINGS

Studying Biodiversity
Among Ecosystems

Explore how environmental factors shape the *biodiversity*—the variety of life—in ground litter (accumulated organic material between the ground and root system of plants) ecosystems in the following project:

What you need:

plastic bags
thermometer
psychrometer (see Figure 2-1)
Berlese apparatus (see Figure 2-2)
trowel
tape measure
4 pencils
bottle of water
camel's hair brush,
    eyedropper
small observation dish
magnifying glass
    or stereomicroscope

What to do:

1. Locate two different ecosystems near where you live; for example, a lawn litter ecosystem, forest litter ecosystem, bare ground ecosystem, flower bed litter ecosystem, or sidewalk crack ecosystem.

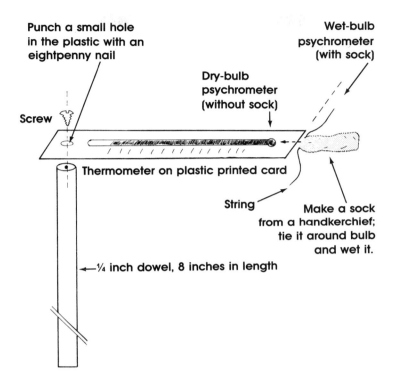

Punch a small hole in the plastic with an eightpenny nail

Wet-bulb psychrometer (with sock)

Dry-bulb psychrometer (without sock)

Screw

Thermometer on plastic printed card

String

Make a sock from a handkerchief; tie it around bulb and wet it.

¼ inch dowel, 8 inches in length

Figure 2-1   Making a Psychrometer

Construct two dry-bulb psychrometers as shown. Attach a "sock" to one of the thermometers with a string to make a wet-bulb psychrometer. To determine the relative humidity: wet the sock of the wet-bulb psychrometer. Swing the psychrometer around on its rod for approximately 2 minutes; then read the thermometer. Repeat with the dry-bulb psychrometer. Record both data points in your notebook. On the chart on the next page, look up the dry-bulb temperature and the difference between wet-bulb and dry-bulb readings; the number at the intersection of the two values is the relative humidity as a percent.

RELATIVE HUMIDITY CHART

Dry Bulb Temperature (°C)	Differences Between Dry-Bulb and Wet-Bulb Temperatures													
	0.5	1.0	1.5	2.0	2.5	3.0	3.5	4.0	4.5	5.0	5.5	6.0	6.5	7.0
10	94	88	82	77	71	66	60	55	50	44	39	34	29	24
11	94	89	83	78	72	67	61	56	51	46	41	36	32	27
12	94	89	83	78	73	68	63	58	53	48	43	39	34	29
13	95	89	83	79	74	69	64	59	54	50	45	41	36	32
14	95	90	84	79	75	70	65	60	56	51	47	42	38	34
15	95	90	85	80	75	71	66	61	57	53	48	44	40	36
16	95	90	85	81	76	71	67	63	58	54	50	46	42	38
17	95	90	86	81	76	75	68	64	60	55	51	47	43	40
18	95	91	86	82	77	73	69	65	61	57	53	49	45	41
19	95	91	87	82	78	74	70	65	62	58	54	50	46	43
20	96	91	87	83	78	74	70	66	63	59	55	51	48	44
21	96	91	87	83	79	75	71	67	64	60	56	53	49	46
22	96	92	87	83	80	76	72	68	64	61	57	54	50	47
23	96	92	88	84	80	76	72	69	65	62	58	55	52	48
24	96	92	88	84	80	77	73	69	66	62	59	56	53	49
25	96	92	88	84	81	77	74	70	67	63	60	57	54	50
26	96	92	88	85	81	78	74	71	67	64	61	58	54	51
27	96	92	89	85	82	78	75	71	68	65	62	58	56	52
28	96	93	89	85	82	78	75	72	69	65	62	59	56	53
29	96	93	89	86	82	79	76	72	69	66	63	60	57	54
30	96	93	89	86	83	79	76	73	70	67	64	61	58	55
31	96	93	90	86	83	80	77	73	70	67	64	61	59	56
32	96	93	90	86	83	80	77	74	71	68	65	62	60	57
33	97	93	90	87	83	80	77	74	71	68	66	63	60	57
34	97	93	90	87	84	81	78	75	72	69	66	63	61	58
35	97	94	90	87	84	81	78	75	72	69	67	64	61	59

7.5	8.0	8.5	9.0	9.5	10.0	10.5	11.0	11.5	12.0	12.5	13.0	13.5	14.0	14.5	15.0
20	15	10	6												
22	18	13	9	5											
25	21	16	12	8											
28	23	19	15	11	7										
30	26	22	18	14	10	6									
32	27	24	20	16	13	9	6								
34	30	26	23	19	15	12	8	5							
36	32	28	25	21	18	14	11	8							
38	34	30	27	23	20	17	14	10	7						
39	36	32	29	26	22	19	16	13	10	7					
41	37	34	31	28	24	21	18	15	12	9	6				
42	39	36	32	29	26	23	20	17	14	12	9	6			
44	40	37	34	31	28	25	22	19	17	14	12	9	6		
45	42	39	36	33	30	27	24	21	19	16	12	11	8	6	
46	43	40	37	34	31	29	26	23	20	18	15	13	10	8	5
47	44	41	39	36	33	30	28	25	22	20	17	15	12	10	8
49	46	43	40	37	34	32	29	26	24	21	19	17	14	12	10
50	47	44	41	38	36	33	31	28	26	23	21	18	16	14	12
51	48	45	42	40	37	34	32	29	27	25	22	20	18	16	13
52	49	46	43	41	38	36	33	31	28	26	24	22	19	17	12
52	50	47	44	42	39	37	35	32	30	28	25	23	21	19	17
53	51	48	45	43	40	38	36	33	31	29	27	25	22	20	18
54	51	49	46	44	41	39	37	35	32	30	28	26	24	22	20
55	52	50	47	45	42	40	38	36	33	31	29	27	25	23	21
56	53	51	48	46	43	41	39	37	35	32	30	28	26	24	23
56	54	51	49	47	44	42	40	38	36	34	32	30	28	26	24

2. With the tape measure and pencils, establish a 6-inch-square investigation area for each ecosystem (mark off a 24-inch distance for the sidewalk crack ecosystem).

3. In your field notebook record temperature and relative humidity readings (see Figure 2-1) for each ecosystem at approximately the same time of day and at similar height zones: *surface* (1 to 3 inches above the surface), middle (12 inches), and high (3 feet).

4. Use a trowel to collect litter material from the 6-inch-square area (or 24-inch length crack space) of each investigated ecosystem. Place collected material in two separate plastic bags.

5. Set up a Berlese apparatus (see Figure 2-2) for each ecosystem investigated.

6. Examine collected specimens from each litter by placing them on sheets of white or black construction paper and using a magnifying glass or stereomicroscope. Use an artist's brush to retrieve and manipulate delicate organisms for examination. It is not necessary for you to identify any collected organism; simply group together like organisms and report each group as a *taxon* (a taxonomic group of any rank or size). You do not have to know what each organism is, only that each group has identical individuals.

7. For each ecosystem studied, compile these data in your field notebook:

— Temperature and relative humidity for each of the three height zones.
— Number of taxons and number of organisms per taxon.

8. Calculate the Diversity Index for each studied ecosystem, using the formula and the hypothetical example on the next page.

$$\text{Diversity} = \frac{N\,(N-1)}{\Sigma n\,(n-1)}$$

N = total number of individuals of all species

n = number of individuals of a species (taxon)

Σ means sum

Example:

Ecosystem 1: Sidewalk Crack

Taxon 1   96
Taxon 2   4

Ecosystem 2: Forest Litter

Taxon 1   20
Taxon 2   3
Taxon 3   30
Taxon 4   37
Taxon 5   10

$$\frac{100(100-1)}{96(96-1)} = \frac{9900}{9132} = 1.08$$
$$+$$
$$4(4-1)$$

$$\frac{100(100-1)}{20(20-1)} = \frac{9900}{2678} = 3.70$$
$$+$$
$$3(3-1)$$
$$+$$
$$30(30-1)$$
$$+$$
$$37(37-1)$$
$$+$$
$$10(10-1)$$

In this example, Ecosystem 2 (forest litter) with a Diversity Index of 3.07 is more diverse than Ecosystem 1, (litter in a sidewalk crack), which has a Diversity Index of 1.08.

Use your data to answer the following:

— At each height zone—surface, middle, and high—which ecosystem is coolest and most humid; warmest and least humid?

— At which height zone are these ecosystems most alike in temperature and humidity?

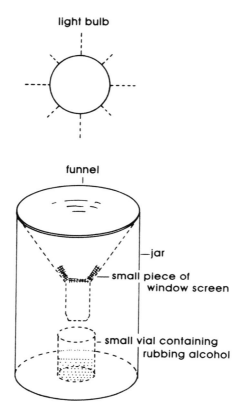

light bulb

funnel

jar

small piece of window screen

small vial containing rubbing alcohol

Figure 2-2   Berlese Apparatus

Place ground litter into the funnel and position a 25-watt bulb 2 inches above the funnel. As the ground litter dries out, organisms inhabiting it will migrate to lower levels of the cone to escape the heat coming from the bulb. Eventually, they will fall through the neck of the funnel into the jar filled with rubbing alcohol. Keep flames and sparks away from the alcohol because it is flammable. The alcohol kills and preserves the organisms, making identification possible. Each sample of ground litter should be "processed" in the apparatus for at least 24 hours.

— Which ecosystem experiences the greatest temperature and humidity fluctuations?

— Would the life-forms collected within one ecosystem survive in the other?

— Would a rain shower or other climatic condition or event impact each ecosystem differently?

GETTING TO KNOW MICROLIFE

Bacteria, Fungi, and Protists

Microlife is the silent engine powering the biosphere: some are *producers,* making their own food, some are *decomposers,* converting dead organic material to more of itself, and some are *consumers,* feeding upon other organisms or their wastes. Microlife play a vital role in food webs by transforming inorganic materials into complex organic compounds eaten by other organisms. Animals and plants would soon die if microbes became extinct. The following projects introduce you to inhabitants of the "World of Little" and ways to know them better.

VIEWING THE SUBVISIBLE WORLD—
CULTURING AND STAINING BACTERIA

• Because most bacteria cannot be seen unless they are in large groups, you will have to provide a suitable microhabitat for them to grow and flourish. Boiled carrots are an excellent growth medium for many types of bacteria.

To make carrot media, cut carrot pieces and boil them for 20 minutes. Pour off water and carrot pieces into a strainer. Allow carrots to cool. Use kitchen tongs to place boiled carrots on some dampened towels in a shallow bowl. "Inoculate" your media (in several bowls) by touching or sprinkling the surface of boiled carrots with cotton swabs previously run over various household or outdoor surfaces (even soil). Inoculate one surface per bowl. Once they are inoculated, cover with clear food wrap and let "incubate" at room temperature for one to five days.

— What kinds of colony growth do you see? Do colonies appear fuzzy, wet, or shiny; are they different colors from reds to creams to off-whites? (The fuzzy growths are fungi; use the Key in this chapter as an aid in identification.)

— Try other culture media such as milk left open to air at room temperature and boiled foods such as potatoes and apples.

— Use a cotton applicator to swab water samples from ponds, puddles, and other sources onto cooked carrot or potato medium (one medium "bowl" per swabbed surface) to determine which microhabitat (inside the home versus outdoors, or one room compared with another) is the more diverse.

• If you have access to a microscope, study individual bacteria cells taken from these colonies. To observe individual bacteria cells, you will need to stain them on a microscope slide. Your science teacher should have access to either crystal violet or methylene blue stain (0.1 percent). Use Figure 2-3 as a guide to the staining procedure outlined next:

Caution: **Wear eye goggles, protective gloves, and an apron or smock when working with stains.**

1. Use a medicine dropper to add a drop of water to the center of a clean glass slide.

2. Use the point of a toothpick to pick up a very small amount of material from a particular bacteria colony. Mix the material with a water drop on the slide to create a smear. Rub the contaminated end of the toothpick into a paper towel moistened with rubbing alcohol—Caution: FLAMMABLE LIQUID— AVOID OPEN FLAMES AND SPARKS—to decontaminate it before discarding.

3. Allow the water drop to air dry.

4. Use a clothespin to hold the slide. Flood the smear with drops of crystal violet or methylene blue stain. Let stand 5 to 10 seconds.

5. Rinse off the stain under a gently dripping faucet. Allow the slide to air dry. Wash your hands thoroughly.

6. Observe the slide under a compound microscope at high-dry magnification (X430). Look for various shapes: rods, spheres, or spirals. Many times bacteria cells will be in groups (chains or packets).

BIOREMEDIATION ON HOME TURF

There are many commercially available products at lawn and garden centers that contain bacterial strains designed to aid in "natural recycling"—from prevention of clogging of septic tanks and soap digestion in septic lines to composting and dethatching. Visit a store near you and purchase a "natural" lawn dethatching product that breaks down dead grass—thatch—accumulating around root systems. Try this project to learn more about *bioremediation*, using an organism to alter an environmentally negative effect.

   • Mark two 5-foot-square plots in a lawn needing dethatching. Bury clean glass microscope slides, randomly spaced at various depths from root level to 10 inches. Try not to disturb thatch areas; replace sod exactly as found. Mark slide locations with sticks. Prepare and apply commercial dethatcher as directed to one plot, nothing to the other. Recover slides after a minimum of 4 weeks and stain following the directions given previously.

   — Compare and contrast bacterial populations in terms of the number, shape, and size of soil bacteria within a plot and between test plots. Use the biodiversity project earlier in this chapter to determine which plot has a more diverse bacterial population. Is there a difference in the amount of lawn thatch material? How effective is the product you used?

STALKING THE WILD FUNGUS

You are probably familiar with mushrooms, but what you see and eat is just the *reproductive* part of the fungus itself. The rest of

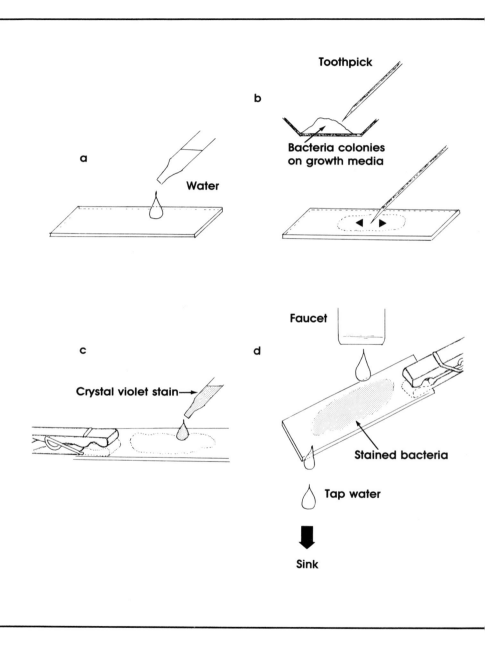

a Water

b Toothpick

Bacteria colonies
on growth media

c Crystal violet stain

d Faucet

Stained bacteria

Tap water

Sink

the fungus lies hidden underground in the form of a netlike or cottonlike mass called *mycelia*, which is made up of slender, interwoven, hairlike tubes called *hyphae*. Mycelia of one fungus, *Armillaria bulbosa*, is estimated to be over a millennium in age; the network of mycelia is said by scientists to extend underground over 38 acres! Here are a few activities to acquaint you better with fungi—nature's scavengers:

• Carefully expose the *outlying root hair systems near the surface* of almost any wild plant, particularly pine and spruce trees. This is the mycorrhizal zone. Remove part of the plant's root system including small clumps of soil and place it on top of some black construction paper in strong light. Use a pocket lens to view the mycorrhizal zone—an area of close association between fungal mycelia and plant root systems. You will observe the tiny transparent or whitish threads of fungal mycelia, or mycorrhizal fungi, at work. This intricate network—"fungus root"—aids in nutrient uptake for its partner plant.

Figure 2-3   Staining Bacteria
(a) Apply a drop of water to a clean microscope slide. (b) With a toothpick, pick up a tiny portion of a bacterial or fungal colony growing on growth media or on foods. Create a smear by mixing the material with the water drop on the slide and letting it dry. (Rub the contaminated end of the toothpick into a paper towel moistened with rubbing alcohol to decontaminate it before discarding.) (c) Hold the slide with a clothespin while you apply crystal violet stain. Apply the stain drop by drop until you create a puddle on the slide. (d) After a minute, rinse the stain away over the sink by allowing drops of water to fall on the slide. Let the slide dry. Observe under a compound microscope at high power (430X).

- Scientists are just beginning to learn that mycorrhizal fungi are sensitive to high levels of nitrogen from car exhausts and ammonia fertilizers. Go hunting for mushroom patches. Establish 100 square foot plots and count the frequency of mushrooms or mycelia you encounter around various plant root systems inside the plots. Also take soil-nitrogen readings using a soil test kit (available at local garden centers). Try to sample in areas where road traffic and/or fertilizer application is heavy. Also sample in wooded areas away from urban disturbances to determine whether excess nitrogen is affecting fungal populations.

- Look for more mushrooms. Take along a penknife and a hand lens. Search for mushrooms in meadows, in dark moist places, on rotting logs, on lawns after a rain, or on compost heaps. Use the penknife carefully to move soil away from the mushroom's stalk (*stipe*) to expose the cottonlike mycelia. Maybe you will discover another giant mycelium!

- Travel into a local wooded area and try to observe "white rot"—a remarkable white fungus that grows on dead trees and degrades lignin, an insoluble biopolymer in trees, to get to its favorite food, cellulose. When it is starved for nitrogen, the fungus secretes a very powerful enzyme (ligninase) to break down lignin, one of the substances that give woody plants their structural support. Environmental scientists are working to adapt this voracious appetite to creosote and pentachlorophenol (PCP)—two toxic wood preservatives at various Environmental Protection Agency (EPA) Superfund sites.

- Fungi have three main goals in life: (1) to convert their food into more of themselves, (2) to reproduce, and (3) to convert their food into chemicals that will discourage you or other organisms, including other fungi, from eating this food. Use the following dichotomous (two-statement) key to identify fungi commonly observed around the home.

Key to Fungus Types

1a If there are fuzzy growth areas colored black, white, and/or gray, **go to 2.**

1b If there are fuzzy growth areas colored yellow or blue-green, **go to 4.**

2a If, under the magnifying glass, the hyphae (cottonlike mass) are not readily visible and there are numerous small spheres, the fungus is *Aspergillus flavus.*

2b If, under the magnifying glass, a white to gray cotton mass is seen, **go to 3.**

3a If the hyphae are beige-white and black spheres are observed, the fungus is *Mucor.*

3b If the hyphae are gray to white and black spheres are observed, the fungus is *Rhizopus.*

4a If the hyphae (cottonlike mass) are yellow with numerous black spheres, the fungus is *Aspergillus niger.*

4b If the hyphae are blue-green to gray and few if any dark spheres are observed, the fungus is *Penicillium.*
    • Calculate species diversity indices for various moldy fruits, vegetables, and breads to find out whether fungi really are exclusionary in staking out their meals.

VIEWING THE "WORLD OF LITTLE"

> *Here, Gentleman, you have the notes that I have kept about my observations: in making which I said to myself, how many creatures are still unbeknown to us, and how little do we yet understand!*
> —*Antony van Leeuwenhoek*
> *Letter 18; October 9, 1676*

Leeuwenhoek was the eighteenth-century Dutch micronaturalist who first described bacteria, protists, and myriad other microlife forms in letters written to the Royal Society of London. He crafted over 500 single-lens microscopes, and his observations are as clear and intriguing today as when penned more than 300 years ago. His letters reveal a unique, animated curiosity in exploration—of microenvironments ranging from the human mouth to bird baths!

This "World of the Little" is all around us, and in us—anyplace that contains water. To view this inner-space world, you will need either a single-lens or a compound (many lenses) microscope. Use Figure 2-4 as your guide in identifying some of the "wee beasties" you will encounter in:

• Living water—collect standing water from sources near where you live—puddles, gutters, ditches, ponds. Make wet-mounts for study under a compound microscope. (To make a wet mount, place a drop of water to be examined in the center of a glass microscope slide; then, to avoid capturing bubbles, gently lower a coverslip [at a 45-degree angle] onto the drop.) Use the biodiversity project earlier in this chapter to determine which microhabitat is the most diverse.

• Living green—*Protococcus* is a green protist found growing as a green film on any moist surface outdoors—tree bark,

Figure 2-4   Microlife Forms
To identify life-forms, compare what you see under the microscope to these forms. The cyanobacteria (blue-green algae) are: (1) Anacystis, (2) Oscillatoria, (3) Phormidium, and (22) Spirulina. The protists, which include protozoans and many kinds of algae, are: (4) Ankistrodesmus, (5) Chlorella, (6) Chlamydomonas, (7) Closterium, (8) Cyclotella, (9) Gomphonema, (10) Lepocinclis, (11) Euglena, (12) Melosira, (13) Navicula, (14) Nitzschia, (15) Micratinium, (16) Pandorina, (17) Scenedesmus, (18) Phacus, (19) Synedra, (20) Micrasterias, (21) Hydrodictyon, (23) Stigeoclonium, and (24) Haematococcus.

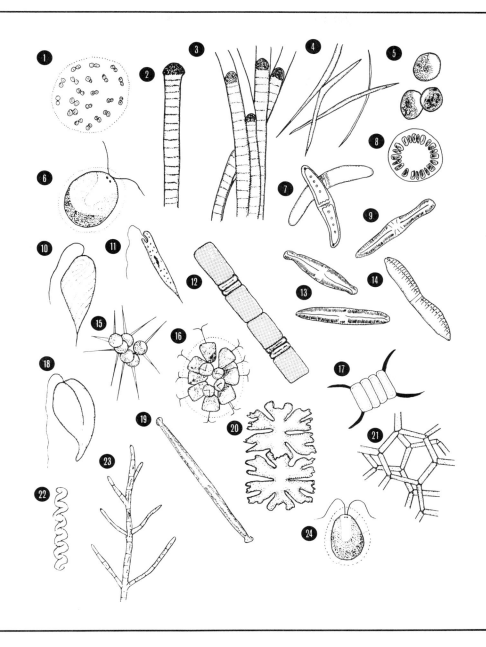

rocks, and concrete. Do you find *Protococcus* growing on surfaces mostly facing a particular direction? Could it be used as a biological compass?

• Infusions—Explore the "World of Little" at your leisure by creating a miniature microlife ecosystem in a jar! Place a handful of finely chopped, dried grass clippings in a mason jar. Add distilled or bottled spring water (available at grocery stores) and allow it to stand on a windowsill that receives northern light. In a week's time, make wet mounts for study with a microscope or use the eye of a canvas needle (available at sewing centers) to sample your infusion for examination with a magnifying glass. Use Figure 2-4 as a guide in identifying various microlife forms.

GETTING TO KNOW PLANTS

Nature's Photon-Powered
Synthesis Factories

Plants are essential to the biosphere as producers; they use light energy to manufacture complex organic compounds and oxygen from carbon dioxide and water. Environmental factors such as rainfall and temperature determine what types of plants survive in a certain region and thus define the community.

WORLD'S LARGEST ORGANISM?

According to the University of Colorado scientist Dr. Jeffrey Mitton, a 106-acre stand of genetically identical quaking aspens located in the Wasatch Mountains of south-central Utah is the world's largest organism. This stand of aspen is a *clone* (a lineage of genetically identical individuals) or *ramet*—each tree (clone) shares the same root system.

• Look at photographs of autumn aspens in travel guides. See whether you can pick out yellow-colored aspen stands that look like circles on the mountainsides, with the tallest ramets in the center and the shorter ones at the perimeter.

• If all the clones share a single root system, do you suppose that these special groups of aspens change color in the fall at the same time?

STUDYING CLIMATIC EVENTS IN TIME—
DENDROCHRONOLOGY

Dendrochronology is the science of dating climatic events and variations in the environment by comparative study of growth rings in trees and aged wood.

Because of seasonal variations in cell growth in the woody parts of trees, spring wood can be recognized as concentric light rings and summer wood as concentric dark rings. One set of light and dark rings signifies 1 year's growth.

Figure 2-5 shows a slab of red pine that is 25 years old. Growth was rapid during the first few years because of little competition from other plants for sun, water, or nutrients. Later, growth slowed down between the fourth and seventh years because less water (in the form of rainfall or snow melt) was available for spring growth.

As the tree grew, crowding from nearby trees caused the rings to get progressively thinner. The shadows of early branches can still be observed before they died off.

You can use this information to study tree growth and past environmental conditions. Try reading cut tree stumps or logs to reconstruct the age of the tree or the climate during the life of the tree, including such events as fire and insect infestation. Check your findings against data from the National Weather Service (radio), newspaper accounts, reports from local Soil Conservation and U.S. Department of Agriculture offices.

HITTING THE TARGET

Pesticide Application

There are more than 50,000 pesticide mixtures on the market, many available for unrestricted, nonlicensed, application. All too often in the war against invading arthropods, these chemical bullets overshoot their target—reaching pets, water, soil, fish, wildlife, adults, and children. Try these projects to learn more about pesticide application and natural alternatives!

• Misapplication of a pesticide so that it overshoots the target is termed *drift*. Visit a local garden center and identify spray-

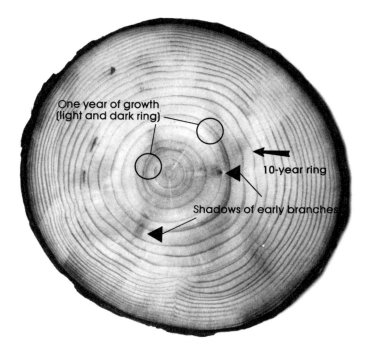

One year of growth
(light and dark ring)

10-year ring

Shadows of early branches

**Figure 2-5   Studying Variation in the Environment—
Dendrochronology**

applied pesticides. Copy down all the ingredients as well as application instructions into your field notebook. Create your own simulated pesticide/herbicide to test: obtain a clean spray bottle and fill it with water to which a heavy concentration of red food coloring has been added.

— Select a series of test areas to simulate a pesticide application (lawn, flower bed, shrubs, etc.). Staple large (3 by 3 feet) pieces of white paper or posterboard to wooden stakes. Position these "drift monitors" between 3 to 6 feet from the application area in four directions (north, east, south, and west). Record wind direction and speed from the weather radio in your field notebook. Apply the simulated test pesticide/herbicide as described by the manufacturer for a commercial product. Do the white paper monitors show evidence of drift?

— Reposition drift monitors to see how far away from the application site the simulated pesticide is carried for that particular set of weather conditions. Repeat the experiment in high wind conditions; is there greater evidence of drift?

— For lawn applications, tape white paper pieces to the sides of your shoes and around your ankles. Many states require that lawn care companies provide written warning signs at the perimeter of lawns treated with pesticides or herbicides. Apply the simulated pesticide/herbicide to an area of lawn, following the manufacturer's instructions for a commercial product. How much simulated pesticide/herbicide do you pick up by "trespassing" on lawns that have had recent pesticide application? With permission, position white socks on your household dog and find out how much simulated pesticide (red dye) is picked up by unleashed animals.

Caution: **Do this project with an adult. Wear a particulate mask when grinding flowers. Never breathe in dust; it is harmful.**

• Pyrethrum is a natural insecticide obtained from chrysanthemum flowers (the active ingredient is chrysanthemummoncarboxylic acid that is chemically extracted from the flowers). Test the effectiveness of ground chrysanthemum flowers on captured flies, mosquitoes, and garden insects. Obtain chrysanthemum flowers and allow them to dry. Use a mortar and pestle to grind flowers into a fine powder.

— Place the ground material in a small pie tin that is, in turn, placed inside a plastic bag. Collect various insects and place them inside the bag. Compare and record the effect of the dried chrysanthemum flowers versus an inert material (talcum powder) inside another plastic bag.

• Visit your local garden center and look for commercial

products containing chemically extracted pyrethrins. Apply a small amount onto a piece of kitchen sponge. Place it with insects inside a plastic bag as before. Is the usefulness of the commercial material greater than your nonextracted (ground-up) material?

A CLOSER LOOK AT

Biological Controls

Biological control is the practice of introducing a natural predator, parasite, or pathogen, which is a disease-causing bacteria or virus, into the environment to regulate a population of specific pests. Worldwide, more than 300 biological pest controls have been established; the following projects let you evaluate the effectiveness of some of them!

• Biological insecticide—Introduced since 1990, one of the safest insecticides on the market, *Bacillus thuringiensis* (BT) produces a crystalline protein endotoxin that causes intestinal paralysis in the larvae of most species of caterpillar-stage insects (mosquito, moth, and butterfly larvae). Visit your local garden center and scan the shelves for products that contain BT. Design some experimental trials that test the effectiveness of the product(s) on collected caterpillars. For example, how low a dose is effective? Does the dose amount differ for terrestrial (butterfly caterpillar) and aquatic application (mosquito larva)?

• *Mail order critters!*—Many garden supply catalogs supply natural predators or parasites that are effective biological controls. Obtain some from the table at the top of the next page and plan an experiment that tests their effectiveness (follow release instructions). For example, you might produce a video documentary that illustrates how pests are reduced after introduction of the control organism.

• *Practicing allelopathy*—Some plants, which are called allelopathic, produce chemicals that are toxic to their weed competitors or that repel or poison their insect pests. Test or observe this phenomenon by planting peppermint around your house to repel ants or investigate the weed-killing ability of ground horse chestnut seed pods by applying them to weeds.

Control Organism	Target Organisms	Release Rate
Ladybug (*Hippodamia convergens*)	Aphids	4,500 per 50 × 50 foot area
Praying mantis (*Tenodera sp.*) egg cases	A wide variety of insects	1 egg case per 100 sq. ft.
Lacewing (*Chrysopa carnea*) egg	Aphids, mealy bugs	1,000 eggs per 500 sq. ft.
Parasitic nematodes	Grub stage of various insects	10 million per 600 sq. ft.

Learn More About It

LAWN CARE — FREE. *Lawn Care Pesticides: A Guide for Action.* New York State Department of Law, Environmental Protection Bureau, Albany, New York. 518/473-3105

BIOPESTICIDES — FREE. *Bacillus thuringiensis—From Beginning to End.* Commonwealth of Pennsylvania, Department of Environmental Resources, Bureau of Forestry, Division of Pest Management, Harrisburg, Pennsylvania.

Read More About It

Bleifield, M. *Experimenting with a Microscope.* New York: Watts, 1988.

Bulloch, William. *The History of Bacteriology.* New York: Dover, 1976.

Dobell, Clifford. *Antony van Leeuwenhoek and His Little Animals.* New York: Dover, 1969.

Gay, Kathlyn. *Cleaning Nature Naturally.* New York: Walker, 1991.

Global Biodiversity Strategy and Global Biodiversity Strategy: A Policy Maker's Guide. Washington, DC: World Resources Institute, 1992.

Jahn, Theodore L., et al. *How to Know the Protozoa.* 2nd ed. Dubuque, Iowa: William C. Brown, 1979.

Lee, Sally. *Pesticides.* New York: Franklin Watts, 1991.

Lincoff, G. H. *The Audubon Society Field Guide to North American Mushrooms.* New York: Knopf, 1981.

Petrovic, Anthony Martin. "Home Lawns." In *Cornell Cooperative Extension Publication Bulletin* 185. Ithaca, N.Y.: Cornell University Press, 1982.

Rainis, Kenneth. *Nature Projects for Young Scientists.* New York: Watts, 1989.

————Exploring with a Magnifying Glass. New York: Watts, 1991.

Sagan, Dorion, and Lynn Margulis. *Garden of Microbial Delights: A Practical Guide to the Subvisible World.* New York: Harcourt Brace Jovanovich, 1988.

Wilson, E. O. *Biodiversity.* Washington, DC: National Academy Press, 1987.

3

RECYCLING
NATURE'S WAY AND OTHERWISE!

In nature there is no waste. Everything is recycled. The ecosphere is a delicate web maintained through the various biogeochemical cycles that transport nutrients from the environment to life forms, then back to the environment.

This chapter provides an opportunity to explore how matter is recycled in ecosystems, and how our efforts mimic that of nature.

THE WATER CYCLE

In the hydrologic cycle, water is collected, purified, and distributed throughout the air, land, and sea, and between living things. Use Figure 3-1 as a visual guide to investigating these dynamic processes within the self-renewing cycle:

• *Transpiration*—the release of water vapor from a plant after water has been absorbed by a plant's root system and transported up the stem to the leaves.

In summer, in an acre of corn the plants will transpire about 325,000 gallons of water during an average growing season!

(1) Transpiration

(2) Evaporation

(3) Cloud formation and precipitation

(4) Surface water runoff

(5) Groundwater

(6) Infiltration

(7) Domestic and industrial use

(8) Aquifer/deep storage

Figure 3-1   The Water Cycle
Water descends from the atmosphere, travels various
pathways on the ground, and then is recycled
back into the atmosphere by the processes shown.

Investigate this process by placing and tying plastic bags over individual plants, or by placing a plastic sheet over a small area of grass. Collect and measure the volume of water vapor condensate to answer the following questions:

— Is transpiration slower during the night or during the day (morning or afternoon)?

— Is transpiration slower on cool, cloudy days than on warm, sunny days?

— Does transpiration increase with rising temperature?

— Do individual leaves transpire more when they are in direct sunlight or in shade?

— Do broader-shaped leaves transpire more than thin leaves with comparable surface area?

• *Evaporation*—the conversion of water to water vapor. Place a known amount of water in a shallow pan. Record temperature and relative humidity values (listen to National Weather Service broadcasts) in your field notebook. Later, measure the volume of water remaining after a 2 to 3 hour period and answer the following questions:

— Is evaporation greater during periods of high or low relative humidity?

— What is the source of most of the atmosphere's moisture?

— Can you devise a method for estimating how much water evaporates from a pond as compared to other water sources?

• *Cloud Formation and Precipitation*—clouds are composed of condensed water vapor. Water droplets in clouds act as miniature diamonds reflecting sunlight to produce the snowy whiteness we see. Become a cloud reader (see Figure 3-2) and use cloud formations to forecast the weather:

Cumulus—formed by convection currents cooling to condensation points at approximately 4,000 feet in altitude. If medium-sized, they mean fair weather; large and low, they mean rain.

Stratus—low, flat clouds usually no higher than 3,000 feet. Almost always associated with precipitation.

Cirrus—featherlike strands at high altitudes (30,000 feet). Composed of ice crystals. If they increase in size, becoming

Cumulus

Cirrus

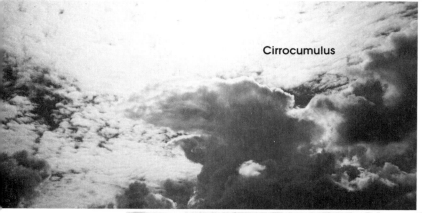

Cirrocumulus

Altocumulus

Stratus

Cumulonimbus

Figure 3-2   Cloud Cues

You can forecast the weather based on the shape and altitude of clouds. Cirrus are high-altitude clouds; altus are middle-altitude clouds; cumulus are clouds in heaps; stratus are clouds in layers; and nimbus are rain clouds. To more precisely describe a cloud, these terms may be combined as a prefix or a suffix with other cloud types as in three of the cloud types shown. Cumulus and cirrus clouds mean fair weather; cirrostratus and cirrocumulus clouds signify a change in the weather; and the clouds that warn of rain are altocumulus, stratus, and cumulonimbus.

cirrostratus, a storm is approaching; if they come and go without changing size, fair weather will continue.

When water droplets combine and grow too large and heavy to stay uplifted, they fall as *precipitation.*

— Learn more about rain and raindrops by studying micro-dough balls: place a layer of finely sifted flour in an aluminum pie pan left out in the open just before it starts to rain. Capture the first raindrops as dough balls for study: Do raindrops vary in size? What is the average size of droplets in drizzle compared to a light rain; a hard rain?

— Water droplets form on tiny particles of matter known as *condensation nuclei.* Use a compound microscope to observe this condensation effect. Breathe (through a plastic straw onto a thin, *cold* 1" by 3" piece of plastic placed under a microscope at X100. Compare your observations to a similar plastic slide that has first been passed through smoke from an extinguished match to catch condensation nuclei.

— Research how rainfall is affected by factors such as latitude, large bodies of water, land features, cities and urban activity.

• *Surface-water runoff and infiltration*—between rainfall and evaporation lies the precarious water balance maintained by plants and the soil ecosystem. See the next chapter to learn more!

THE NITROGEN CYCLE

The flow of nitrogen and its compounds among life-forms and throughout the environment is called the nitrogen cycle. Comprising 78 percent of our atmosphere, nitrogen is an essential component of all living things. Before it can be assimilated, atmospheric nitrogen must be converted by specialized bacteria and other microbes to a form (ammonia [NH_4]), that can be used by plants. Other bacteria convert the ammonia into nitrites and nitrates, nutrients essential for growth. See Figure 3-3.

You can investigate these bacteria using clover, a common

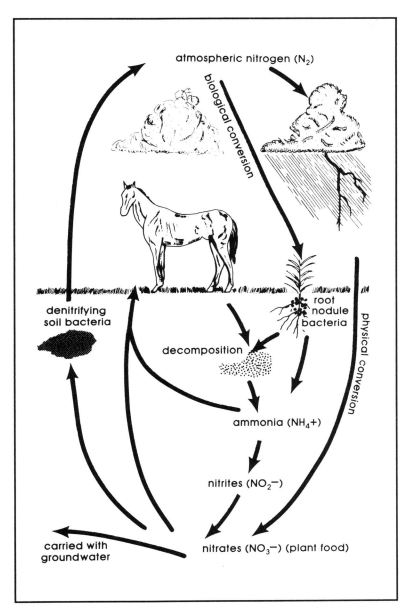

Figure 3-3   The Nitrogen Cycle

plant found along the roadside and in fields. Carefully dig up the clover's root system and wash off the soil. Do you notice any pea-size nodules on the roots?

• Cut a small piece of nodule and crush it between two microscope slides. Separate the slides and stain, using the crystal violet stain described in Chapter 2. Under the compound microscope at X400, or higher magnification if possible, you should observe pockets of rod-shaped bacteria (*Rhizobium trifolium*) in groups of four to eight cells inside a thin membrane (see Figure 3-4).

• Find out whether these bacteria indeed cause nodules. Germinate clover seeds on damp paper towels. When they have developed a root system (1 to 2 inches [2-5] cm in length), place them in a shallow dish of water. Grind 15 to 30 clover nodules and inoculate the young clover plants by mixing the ground nodule material in the seedlings' water. You are inoculating the young clover plants with nitrogen-fixing bacteria contained within the nodules.

— Make a control—boil some of the inoculated clover plants for 30 minutes to kill any bacteria.

— Wait a few days, then plant both groups of plants in sterile potting soil (obtained at a garden center). After 2 to 3 months, dig up the plants and inspect for root nodules. Which are the active ingredients: the nodules themselves or the bacteria inside?

• Use a soil test kit (available at a home garden center) to test for the presence of nitrates in the soil—the product of nitrogen fixation.

THE CARBON CYCLE

Carbon is an integral part of life's fabric and its source is carbon dioxide—free and abundant in the atmosphere and dissolved in the waters of the earth. Use Figure 3-5 as a guide to find out how carbon is cycled. The largest store of carbon on Earth is in limestone as calcium carbonate. Explore various aspects of this unique process by doing these projects:

Figure 3-4
Studying Nitrogen Fixation
Nodules on the roots of leguminous plants, such as peas and beans, contain bacteria that convert nitrogen from the air into plant nutrients.

Legume nodules

Rhizobium trifolium bacteria

LIFE IS A GAS!

• Return carbon dioxide to the atmosphere by adding drops of white vinegar to a marble chip (available at garden centers) placed in a paper cup. Use a magnifying glass to observe the liberation of tiny bubbles of carbon dioxide gas from the reaction of a mild acid with calcium carbonate.

• Use pH paper (see chapter 4 to make your own) to measure the pH of tap water in your home. Record the data in your notebook. Use a soda straw to blow bubbles gently into a glass containing a small amount of tap water. Again, test the pH. Do you notice a difference? Can you write a chemical equation for this reaction? HINT: The end product is carbonic acid (H_2CO_3).

• Fill two mason jars 1 inch from the top with tap water and let it stand for at least 24 hours to dechlorinate. In one jar dissolve a quarter of an alkalizing tablet (available at drug stores). Use pH paper to measure the pH of the water in each jar; record your findings in your notebook. Can you explain why your readings are different?

• Place a single sprig of either *Elodea* or *Ceratophylum* (available in aquarium shops) in each jar. Cover each jar with sealing wrap. Place both jars in a place that will receive strong sunlight or illuminate by using a 100-watt spotlight placed 10 inches (30 cm) from the jar. Observe the leaf surfaces of the plants in both jars and measure pH at 1/2-hour intervals over the next 2 to 3 hours. Do you observe gas bubbles? Can you identify the gas? Which jar shows the most activity? On the basis of your observations, can you fill in the rest of the equation for photosynthesis?

$$3\underline{\hspace{1.5cm}} + 3\ H_2O + \frac{\text{light energy}}{\text{chlorophyll}} \rightarrow C_3H_6O_3 + 3\underline{\hspace{1.5cm}}$$

(gas)(water) $\qquad\qquad\qquad\qquad$ $\begin{pmatrix}\text{3-carbon}\\ \text{sugar}\end{pmatrix}$ (gas)

— On the basis of your investigations, what effect does the reduction of tropical rain forests have on the cycling of carbon?

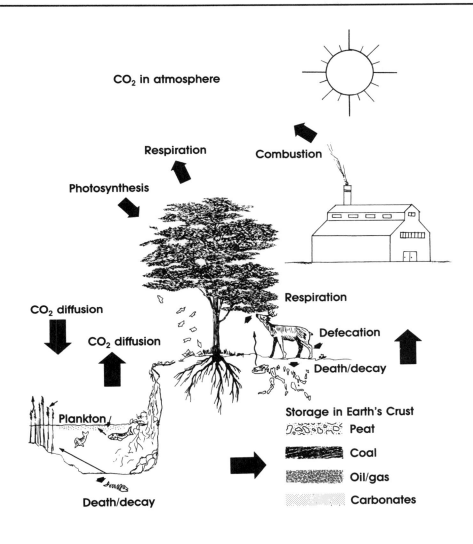

CO₂ in atmosphere

Respiration

Photosynthesis

Combustion

CO₂ diffusion

CO₂ diffusion

Respiration

Defecation

Death/decay

Plankton

Storage in Earth's Crust

Peat

Coal

Oil/gas

Carbonates

Death/decay

Figure 3-5   The Carbon Cycle

WHERE HAS ALL THE CARBON GONE?

Almost 1,000 pounds of carbon a month is released into the atmosphere for every person in the United States! Since the Industrial Revolution of the nineteenth century, atmospheric carbon dioxide levels have increased by about 25 percent. You will learn more about how this gas causes the greenhouse effect in chapter 6. The list below has some interesting carbon statistics that you can use to prepare information charts related to carbon cycling. For example, how many trees must be planted to balance the carbon released by driving 100 miles a week?

• Approximately 0.4 pound of carbon is released into the atmosphere for every kilowatt of energy used.

• A single tree absorbs approximately 36 pounds of carbon from the air each year.

• Approximately 5 pounds of carbon is released for every gallon of gasoline burned in an internal combustion engine.

Source: Adapted from Francesca Lyman, with Irving Mintzer, Kathleen Courier, and James MacKenzie, *The Greenhouse Trap* (Boston: Beacon Press, 1990).

COMPOSTING:
RECYCLING NATURE'S WAY

MAKING COMPOST

1. Locate an area of your yard that provides "mild" sunshine. See Figure 3-6 to learn how to construct a compost facility there.

2. Gather materials to be composted. Be mindful always to maintain a 2:1 mixture of carbon to nitrogen. Generally, fresh green plant material (grass clippings and the like) is high in nitrogen while dried leaves, hay, brush, and stalks are high in carbon.

3. During the first 6 weeks, gently moisten the material, twice a week, using a gentle mist or spray hose setting. Turn your material over completely, using a hoe. Shred the material as you turn it over. (On very hot days you should turn over your pile twice a day to eliminate an odor buildup. Eliminate watering during rainy weeks.)

4. After this initial "run-in period," allow the material to "cure" over a 6-month period to produce a fertilizer that can be added to soil. Compost is ready to use when it is dark brown, crumbly, and earth-smelling. (Generally, a pile started in the summer or fall should be ready for use in the following spring.)

TAKING THE PULSE OF THE PILE
A compost pile is really a recycling factory in miniature. Within, microbes repackage organic and inorganic nutrients locked within the cellular structure of yard waste into usable forms that plants require.

• Monitor the temperature at various depth levels in the pile. Plot and compare temperature readings to those obtained outdoors. Are all levels of the pile equally warmer or colder than outside conditions? Do temperature changes increase when measurements are taken a couple of hours after the pile is turned?

• After the initial "run-in period" bury some 1" by 3" glass microscope slides at various locations within the pile (see Figure 3-6). Try not to disturb these areas for at least 6 to 8 weeks. Afterward, carefully remove the glass slides and stain them according to the directions in Chapter 2. Observe the slides under high-dry magnification (X430) of a compound microscope. Compile a Diversity Index (see Chapter 2) for microlife you observe at various depths within the pile; in areas both nearer the outside of the pile (hence nearer to oxygen) or toward the inside of the pile; at various time periods during compost development.

• Use a soil test kit (available at lawn care centers) to analyze the nutrient content of your finished product. Does it have measurable amounts of phosphorus, nitrogen, and other nutrients? What is its pH?

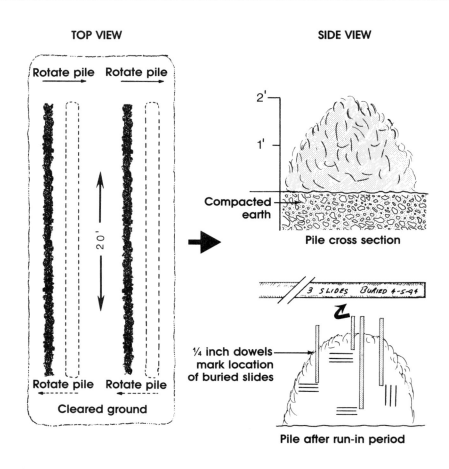

TOP VIEW

Rotate pile　Rotate pile

20'

Rotate pile　Rotate pile

Cleared ground

SIDE VIEW

2'

1'

Compacted
earth

Pile cross section

3 SLIDES BURIED 4-5-94

¼ inch dowels
mark location
of buried slides

Pile after run-in period

Figure 3-6　Constructing a Compost Pile

Build a compost pile on a piece of ground as shown, using a
mixture of fresh green plant cuttings and dried plants in a ratio
of about 2 to 1. Moisten the pile and turn it over completely,
moving it to an adjacent spot as shown, about twice a week for
the first six weeks. Bury microscope slides in the pile after this
run-in period. Without disturbing the pile, examine the slides for
microlife after six to eight weeks.

• Use a Berlese apparatus (Figure 2-2) to capture and examine the small invertebrates in your compost.

RECYCLING BY FIRE!

Exploring Fire Ecology

Forest fires release many nutrients tied up in organic matter, principally potash (potassium carbonate), phosphorus, and nitrogen.

• Investigate just how these nutrients are released by mixing ⅓ cup of compacted fire ash from a wood-burning stove or fireplace with ⅔ cup of coniferous forest soil. This broadly mimics what you would likely observe in soils involved with a recent burn. Use a soil test kit (available at garden supply stores) to determine nitrogen, phosphorus and potash levels as well as pH; compare the results with those from forest soil without the ash.

• Many coniferous species, like the lodgepole pine (*Pinus contorta*) in the West, and the pitch pine (*Pinus rigida*) in the East, use a special type of seed cone—in concert with fire to distribute seeds. These pinecones, called serotinous cones, are covered with a resin that must be softened by high heat before cone scales open to release the seeds.

— If possible, collect serotinous cones (or purchase them from a biological supply house) and investigate how they open and release their seeds:

— Wrap cones in plastic wrap and place in a microwave oven for 1 to 5 minutes (try 1-minute intervals at a "high" power setting until seeds are released). Or use a conventional oven and wrap cones in aluminum foil, start with a cold oven, and heat to 350° for 30 to 45 minutes. Count the seeds from each cone. Use the prepared "ash-soil," described earlier, to see whether released seeds will germinate.

HOW WELL DO YOU KNOW TRASH AND GARBAGE?

In the United States, we generate more solid waste per capita than any other country on Earth. On average, the Environmental

Protection Agency (EPA) estimates that each of us generates more than 4 pounds of waste per day—over 180 million tons.

Rejected materials—*refuse*—is generally classified as either trash or garbage. *Garbage* is refuse resulting from the preparation and cooking of food. It is rich in reduced carbon compounds, in which carbon is bound to hydrogen, nitrogen, and oxygen. *Trash* is refuse containing woody, fibrous or vegetable matter—leaves, grass clippings, wood, wood products, cotton clothing—almost any discarded article. In most trash material, carbon is tightly bound to carbon in linear fashion; items made of glass or metal have little or no carbon.

Neither trash nor garbage disappears once it leaves your home. Investigate what happens to your and your community's trash and garbage:

• With adult permission, conduct a "refuse audit" of your household waste for 1 week. Record all your findings in your notebook. Be sure to wear protective gloves when handling any refuse. See whether the members of your household fit the profile of the average American in terms of what is disposed of each day.

— Separate refuse into the following categories: paper, glass, metals, plastics, rubber, and leather, textiles, wood, and food wastes (garbage). To make sorting easier and cleaner, use a plastic bag for each category.

— Use a bathroom scale (or similar device) to get a *rough* estimate of weight in each category.

— For each category, record an estimate of volume in cubic feet. (Cubic volume = length × width × height.)

— For each category calculate the average daily output per person, per day, in your household:

$$\frac{\text{Total weight}}{7 \text{ days}} = \text{weight/day}$$

$$\frac{\text{weight/day}}{\substack{\text{number of} \\ \text{family members}}} = \text{category weight/person}$$

Waste Materials	Pounds per person per day (1988)
Paper	1.60
Glass	0.28
Metals	0.34
Plastics	0.32
Rubber/leather	0.10
Textiles	0.09
Wood	0.14
Food wastes (garbage)	0.29

Compare your numbers with the EPA figures listed above for waste generated before recycling or incineration.

— Now subtract the weight of items or material that is recycled or could be recycled by your household. Compare the percentages of nonrecyclable materials to those below; these materials usually account for the largest share of landfilled waste:

Paper	40%
Glass	7%
Plastics	8%
Metals	9%
Garbage	25%
Other	11%

AGELESS FIBER

Recycling Paper

Most people assume that paper has always been made from trees. But only since the 1850s have trees been cut and pulped to make paper. For most of its history, paper has been a recycled product!

The first paper, invented in China in A.D. 105, was made from reclaimed material—rags, discarded fishnets—as well as hemp and grass. In 1690, in Philadelphia, recycled rags were used to make paper.

Today's recycled paper is made from wastepaper gener-ated by paper mills, envelope makers, print shops, homes, and businesses. If wastepaper has ink on it, it must be "deinked" to separate contaminants from the paper's fibers. The prepared fibers can then be made into new paper. A rule of thumb in recycling paper is that a ton of paper made from 100 percent wastepaper, rather than from virgin fiber, saves approximately 17 trees, 4,000 kilowatt hours (enough energy to power an average home for 6 months), 7,000 gallons of water, 60 pounds of air-polluting effluents, and 3 cubic yards of landfill space.

Investigate the process by making recycled paper on your own!

What you need:

white scrap paper (office and printing paper; not newsprint)
staples, tacks
2 wooden frames, suggested dimensions 4 by 5 inches
nylon fly screening
kitchen cloths (at least 4)
plastic washtub
mayonnaise jar
blender
wooden spoon
sponge
iron

What to do:

Use the following instructions and Figure 3-7 as a guide to how paper is recycled:

1. First you must make a paper mold. Tack or staple fly screening tightly to frame as shown.

2. *Paper sorting:* Select and use only white, uninked scrap pa-per and remove any plastic or staples.

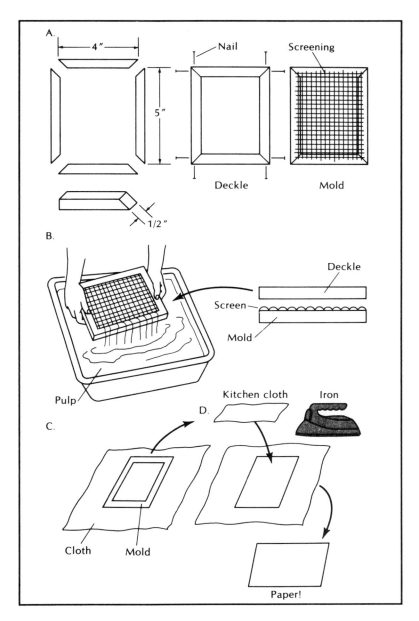

Figure 3-7   Recycling Paper

3. *Vatting:* Tear it into very small pieces (about ½-inch square) and allow it to soak in a mayonnaise jar filled with very hot water for half an hour. The jar will serve as what is called the vat in the recycling process. (NOTE: Allow the water to cool to a temperature that allows for comfortable hand immersion before going to Step 4.)

4. *Pulping:* Take one handful of the soaked paper and place it in a blender about half full of warm water. The blender will be your pulper. Blend at a moderate speed until you can no longer see individual pieces of paper. If you have problems, remove some paper. This recycled fiber is sometimes called secondary fiber because the fibers were already processed (using caustic chemicals to break down wood lignins) when the original paper was pulped.

5. *Pulp refining:* Pour the pulp into a washtub full of warm water. Use a wooden spoon to stir the pulp (this mechanical refining process makes paper fibers more flexible) for 10 to 15 minutes. Increasing or decreasing the amount of pulp will affect the thickness of the paper.

6. *Sheet formation:* Place the second, uncovered wood frame, called a deckle, on top of your screen. With both hands, dip the mold into the tub and scoop up some pulp. Gently shake the mold back and forth to get an even layer of fibers on the screen. When water has drained completely through the mold, carefully remove the deckle, leaving the just-formed sheet on the screen.

7. To remove the paper from the screen, lay a clean kitchen cloth on a flat surface such as a table, then take the screen and lay it face down on the cloth. Soak up any residual moisture from the *back* of the screen with a sponge. Very *gently* lift the screen; the paper should remain on the cloth.

8. *Heat-drying:* To dry the paper, cover it with a kitchen cloth and iron it at a medium-dry setting. Once it is dry, pull gently on either side of the cloth to stretch it. This will soon loosen the paper from the cloth. Gently peel the paper off. *Do not pour the remainder of the pulp down the sink—it might block the drain!* The strained pulp can be thrown out or kept in a plastic bag in the freezer for next time.

Try some variations in the process to illustrate some of the environmental issues concerning paper recycling:

• Manufacturers use secondary fiber to make paperboard, some printed papers, paper napkins, and toweling. Recycle separate "batches" of paper, each containing 100 percent of the following paper types: brown grocery bag paper, white "coated" (shiny) papers, and colored papers.

Caution: **Do not use newsprint or papers with ink printing; some inks contain toxic materials.**

Use the recycling process to help clarify the following environmental issues:

— Use a magnifying glass to learn whether recycled grocery bag paper is dyed brown or is made of unprocessed wood fiber. Do you think that this type of paper could be mixed with other "fine" (office) papers, or must it be sorted? Go to the library or your local county recycling center to learn which of the two paper types versus has more recycling value.

— Did you have difficulty in making recycled paper from coated wastepaper? Coated paper has China clay (a fine white clay called kaolin) incorporated into it. You probably noticed that this pulp is far more lumpy than other pulp types. Research how this material is removed from secondary fiber in the pulping process at a recycling mill. Also find out why this type of paper is often excluded in recycling programs. HINT: Compare the weight of 500 sheets of coated paper stock with that of uncoated stock of similar size.

— Colored paper must be specially processed to remove dyes from secondary fibers. In some cases, recyclers will not accept the ubiquitous "yellow legal sheet" paper because stricter environmental controls on process effluents make its recycling uneconomical. Generally, chlorine is used as a part of this process, raising a concern that additional environmental toxins are produced through its use. Test how well chlorine and hydrogen peroxide work in removing fiber dyes by immersing punched paper circles into separate plastic jug caps, one containing bleach and the other a 3 percent hydrogen peroxide solution.

Caution: Wear protective gloves and safety goggles when working with any chemical solution. Do this investigation under adult supervision. Never mix bleach and hydrogen peroxide solutions.

— Find out how many times paper fiber can be recycled. Recycle selected batches of various paper types: 100 percent rag paper, fine white office paper, brown grocery bag paper, other types.

— Go to stationery stores and read labels affixed to bulk packages of paper used for printing, xerography, and other commercial uses. Read the watermarks in papers; more and more manufacturers are imprinting fiber and recycling content in the watermarks of their papers. How much "postconsumer" fiber is incorporated into these papers? In light of the term *postconsumer*, does *recycled* always have the same meaning?

WHAT DOES *RECYCLED* REALLY MEAN?

Responsible Environmental Advertising

As consumers demand products that are safer for or have a less harmful impact on the environment, industry will strive to meet that demand. Unfortunately, attempts to take advantage of consumers' increasing interest in the environment have led some companies to make environmental advertising claims, known as "Green" marketing, that are trivial, confusing, and misleading.

For example, you may think the label "Recycled Paper" means that the paper contains some portion (maybe even 100 percent) postconsumer fibers. It may not be so: paper manufacturers routinely recycle "mill broke" or scrap (also called *wastepaper*) produced in the papermaking process; it is in all the paper they produce. Therefore, all paper could be classified as "recycled." (Currently, the EPA guideline allows some mill wastepaper to be classified as recycled paper content even when it's used in paper without a single postconsumer fiber.)

The National Association of Attorneys General has formed a task force that called on the federal government to work with states to develop uniform standards for environmental advertising. *The Green Report II* makes recommendations that, if followed by industry, should greatly reduce consumer confusion about environmentally related advertising claims.

• Consult reference sources to help you establish a uniform definition for terms such as *degradable, compostable, environmentally friendly, recycled*, and *recyclable*. Use these created definitions as a guide in determining whether the meaning of the term is radically different when it is used in advertising.

• Canvass stores and read product labels and observe package containers to see whether products meet task force recommendations published in *The Green Report II*:

Recycled—"only postconsumer materials should be referred to as recycled. Recaptured factory material should be referred to as *reprocessed/recovered* material."

Degradable, biodegradable, and *photodegradable*—"products currently disposed of primarily in landfills or through incineration—whether plastic or paper—should not be promoted as *degradable, biodegradable*, or *photodegradable*."

Recyclable—"unqualified recyclability claims should not be made for products sold nationally unless a significant amount of the product is being recycled everywhere the product is sold."

• Find out whether products (such as herbicides and pesticides) advertised as "EPA-registered" are endorsed, tested, analyzed, and approved by the EPA.

• Visit stationery stores and survey the types of papers having "postconsumer content." Is a postconsumer content of 20 percent or greater rare?

MONOMERS OF MANY COLORS

Recycling Plastics

Recently, the EPA estimated that each of us contributes over 116 pounds of plastic to the waste heap yearly. Of concern to environmentalists and industrialists alike is not how to reuse plastics, but how to recycle them—make milk jugs back into milk jugs and soda bottles back into soda bottles—as we now do with aluminum and glass containers.

Since 1979, nine states have followed Michigan's lead in legislating bottle laws designed to recycle plastic, glass, and aluminum beverage containers. What happens to these materials once the deposit money is returned? In the case of plastic soda bottles, they are most likely recycled into a polyester fiber that is sold to manufacturers of carpet, pillows, and ski jackets—but not to make more plastic pop bottles. Usually this "recycling cascade" is limited to only one or two cycles; carpets, for example, are not recyclable. True recycling of plastic is still a long way off.

Choose one or more of these projects to learn more about plastics and recycling:

KNOW THE PLAYERS
The table on the next page lists major plastics and their commercial uses, including what products are made from reused material:

• Conduct a "plastics audit" of materials that your household purchases in the course of a week. Include in your survey the following information:

• Conduct a "plastics audit" of materials that your household purchases during a week's time period. Include in your survey the following information:

— What percentage of all articles had plastic packaging?

Trade Name	Common Use	Current Use of Reused Material
PETE polyethylene terephthalate	Soda bottles	Polyester fiber used in carpets, strapping, paint brushes, scouring pads, fuzz on tennis balls
HDPE high-density polyethylene	Milk/detergent jugs, opaque-colored grocery bags	Detergent/motor oil bottles, plastic lumber, soda bottle bases, combs, trash bags, trash cans, soft drink bottle base cups
PVC polyvinyl chloride	Food wrap, shampoo bottles	Drainage tile, mud flaps, pipes, hoses
LDPE low-density polyethylene	Glossy grocery bags, bread bags, newspaper bags	Garbage bags
PP polypropylene	Jar lids, ketchup bottles, medicine bottles, margarine tubs	Grocery-basket handles, auto batteries, lawn-mower wheels, fast food trays, trays, videocassette storage cases
PS polystyrene	Foamed fast food containers, coffee cups, cutlery	Packing "peanuts," VCR cassettes, desk accessories, insulation

— Which type of plastic material (from the table) was the most prevalent?

— What percentage of plastic was set aside for "recycling"?

• In an effort to assist recycling programs, the Society of the Plastics Industry has developed a coding system (using a three-sided triangular arrow with a number from 1 to 7 in the center, and code letters beneath the number) to identify the resin composition of plastic containers. In some states this code is required on all containers. How many containers from your previous audit have any plastics code? Keep a close watch for each of the seven recyclable code numbers, and use the preceding table to determine each number's material composition. HINT: Number 7 indicates "Other Resins and Layered Multi-material."

• Find out which recycling code numbers are being accepted by recyclers in your community.

EVALUATING THE PLAYERS

• In plastic recycling, mixed plastics are routinely separated in a flotation tank, where some types float and others sink. Collect and categorize various plastics by using the table and place cut pieces of as many types as possible in a pan of water to determine flotation characteristics. Record findings in your notebook.

• In certain cases you can infer that certain products are made from recycled plastic. Usually recycled plastic resin is made from mixed colors and it often is gray-green. Spend some time at local stores to see which articles are made of recycled gray-green plastic. What does the manufacturer state on the label? HINT: Investigate lawn products, trash bags, plastic lumber, and similar products. Can you determine what plastics have been used? Manufacturers also color recycled plastics black to obtain uniform coloration. Can you find examples of these recycled plastics?

• In some instances recycled plastics are covered by virgin material. Try "dissecting" some bottles to discover which are manufactured using this "laminate" system. HINT: Look at empty motor oil containers and certain plastic trash bags.

- Examine products made from different plastic resins (see table) and create a chart of your findings. Be sure to include the following information:
  - General description: Hard/soft? Color? Opaque/transparent?
  - Strength: Can you break it? Does it break? Does it stretch?
  - Uses: Plastic code? What product can it become via recycling?
- Visit a recycling center or materials recovery facility (MRF) near where you live. Write a report that details the mechanics of the recycling process: How are plastic types sorted? What happens to sorted plastic groups? Are these postconsumer plastics truly being recycled?

TRICKLE CHARGE!

Batteries are miniature power-generating stations, producing an electrical current (measured in volts) via an electrochemical reaction. The traditional "single-use" (dry-cell) battery provides a convenient source of portable power that energizes an almost endless variety of devices. According to the EPA, each year we discard over 2.7 billion batteries—and along with them tons of heavy metals such as zinc, copper, and mercury!

- Both disposable dry-cells and nickel-cadmium (Ni-Cad) rechargeable batteries contain toxic heavy metals. Dry-cell manufacturers have made great progress in removing all but a tiny amount of mercury from their products, but approximately 0.1 gram per cell remains and is necessary for the electrochemical reaction. Ni-Cad batteries contain a greater amount of toxics—approximately 22 grams per cell—but because they are rechargeable, far fewer Ni-Cad batteries, are required than dry cells. Which battery type—rechargeables or single-use throwaways—is the more environmentally responsible choice for powering 10 common household items?
- Find out whether a single-use or a rechargeable Ni-Cad battery is cheaper to use in powering a tape deck for a year. Assume that you play tunes 2 hours daily, your deck uses four

batteries, and dry-cells last 5 hours and Ni-Cads last only 2 hours. Visit a local retailer and record current prices to calculate the differences. Factor in additional items: a Ni-Cad charger, $1.50 total energy cost for 365 recharges. How much could your household save if it converted wherever possible from dry-cell to rechargeable?

• Investigate whether your state or town has laws governing the recycling of dry-cell and wet-cell (car, boat) batteries. Use the references at the end of this chapter to find out how battery types can be recycled. Try to estimate the number of pounds of dry-cell batteries disposed of in the trash annually—in your home, in your neighborhood, in your city or town. How are batteries disposed of where you live: in landfills or in incinerators? Can this amount be reduced?

• Calculate how many grams of toxic materials (nickel, mercury, cadmium) your household disposes of yearly.

MAKING A GREEN BATTERY

An electrochemical cell—a battery—produces an electrical current by a chemical reaction. A traditional dry-cell contains two reacting materials (such as carbon and zinc) separated from each other by a conductive pastelike material called an *electrolyte*. In this battery type a carbon rod embedded in a carbon-manganese dioxide mixture is the positive electrode, and the zinc can is the negative electrode. They are separated by a paste containing zinc/ammonium chloride. When the electrodes are connected by an external wire, a path for electrical current is created. This power-generating system is portable and efficient—but also polluting. Let's investigate a natural, nonpolluting power-generating cell—fruit!

To construct your natural power cell insert a straightened paper clip into an apple to a depth of 1 inch. About 3 inches away, insert a piece of copper wire of similar size to the same depth. Attach the negative lead of a voltmeter (available at a local electronics store) to the paper clip and the positive lead to the copper wire. Turn on the voltmeter and set the range to 0 to 5 volts direct current (DC).

• What is the voltage output of your cell? How long will this same output be sustained?

• If you replace the paper clip (a carbon-zinc alloy) with a zinc nail (available at hardware stores), is the voltage output increased?

• Measure the pH of various fruit juices; does pH affect voltage output or performance efficiency? How do you suppose alkaline batteries compare with your natural weak acid battery? What about car batteries? Ask your local mechanic to do a battery pH test for you.

• Which fruit type (pear, lemon, orange, etc.) is the most *efficient* natural voltaic cell—that is, which fruit type generates the highest voltage over the longest period?

• From a local electronics store, obtain a light-emitting diode (LED) having a 1.85-volt (20-mA) power requirement. Calculate how many natural voltaic cells will be required to provide enough current to light the bulb. Assemble your cells and connect them in series: $(+) \rightarrow (-) / (-) \rightarrow (+)$.

INVESTIGATING PHOTOVOLTAICS

From calculators to orbiting satellites, photovoltaic cells, which are charged by sunlight, power an increasing number of electrically powered devices. It is estimated that the sun delivers more energy to Earth daily than the entire Earth's population can use in 36 years. Do these projects to learn more about harnessing this immense power reservoir:

• Obtain some photovoltaic cells from an electronics supply store and hook them up in series. Connect them to a low-voltage LED.

— Determine how many photovoltaics must be placed in the circuit to light the LED using a 60-watt light bulb as an energy source. (You can also use a voltmeter set on its lowest DC setting to measure the current generated by each cell.)

— Place various colored acetate sheets in the light path to observe how the quality of light (its color and/or intensity) affects voltage output. For example, are photovoltaics affected by infrared, ultraviolet, or other visible light spectra?

• Repeat the previous experiment, this time using a parallel circuit: $(+) \rightarrow (+) / (-) \rightarrow (-)$. What differences are noted? Research which circuit type, parallel or series is more often used commercially.

Learn More About It

PAPER   The American Paper Institute's Paper Information Center. Learn more about outlets for wastepaper in your area. Ask for Paper Matcher: *A Directory of Paper Recycling Resources,* a 300-page compendium of recycling mills, paper dealers, and recycling centers across the United States. For your free copy, call 800/878-8878.

PLASTICS   Society of Plastics Industry, 250 Park Ave., New York, NY 10010
American Plastics Council: free booklet telling you more about the benefits of plastic. Call 800/777-9500 Ext. 28.
Center for Plastics Recycling Research, Rutgers, The State University of New Jersey, Busch campus, Bldg. 3529, Piscataway, NJ 08855.

STEEL   Steel Can Recycling Institute, Foster Plaza 10, 680 Anderson Dr., Pittsburgh, PA 15220
American Iron and Steel Institute, 1133 15th Street, N.W., Washington, DC 20005-2701

ALUMINUM   Aluminum: *Alcoa's Guide to Starting Aluminum Can Recycling Activity.* Pittsburgh, PA: Alcoa Recycling Company, November 1988.

Aluminum Association, 818 Connecticut Avenue, NW, Washington, DC 20006.

WORLD	For Free 8″ by 10″ color lithograph contact:
CLOUD	National Aeronautics and Space Administration,
COVER	Goddard Space Center, Greenbelt, MD 20771.
PATTERN	301/286-8955. Ask for document Hql 326.

Read More About It

Alvin, Virginia, and Robert Silverstein. *Recycling: Meeting the Challenge of the Trash Crisis.* New York: Putnam, 1992.

Campbell, Stu. *Let It Rot!: The Gardener's Guide to Composting.* Pownal, Vt.: Storey Publishing, 1990.

Carless, Jennifer. *Taking Out the Trash: A No-Nonsense Guide to Recycling.* Washington, D.C.: Island Press, 1992.

Cullen, Mark, and Lorraine Johnson. *The Urban/Suburban Composter: The Complete Guide to Backyard, Balcony, and Apartment Composting.* New York: St. Martin's Press, 1994.

The Earthworks Group. *The Recycler's Handbook.* Berkeley, Calif.: Earthworks Press, 1990.

Green Report II, The. May 1991. National Association of Attorneys General. Ad Hoc Task Force of Attorneys General for the States of California, Florida, Massachusetts, Minnesota, Missouri, New York, Tennessee, Texas, Utah, Washington, and Wisconsin. (Available from these state attorneys general.)

Heller, J. *Papermaking.* New York: Watson-Guptill, 1978.

Lyman, F., et al. *The Greenhouse Trap.* Boston: Beacon Press, 1990.

Neal, Homer A., and J. R. Schubel. *Solid Waste Management and the Environment: The Mounting Garbage and Trash Crisis.* Englewood Cliffs, NJ: Prentice-Hall, 1987.

Office of Technology Assessment, United States Congress. *New Electric Power Technologies: Problems and Prospects for the 1990's.* Washington, DC: U.S. Government Printing Office, July 1985.

Page, J. *Forest.* Planet Earth series. Alexandria, VA: Time-Life, 1983.

Rainis, Kenneth. Exploring with a Magnifying Glass. New York: Franklin Watts, 1991.

———Nature Projects for Young Scientists. New York: Franklin Watts, 1989.

Romme, W. H., and D. G. Despain. "The Yellowstone Fires." *Scientific American*. 261, 5 (1989): 37–46.

Smith, E. S. *Paper*. New York: Walker, 1984.

Stetoff, Rebecca. *Recycling*. New York: Chelsea House, 1991.

Studley, V. *The Art and Craft of Homemade Paper*. New York: Van Nostrand Reinhold, 1977.

4

LIVING WATER

Water is the medium of life, for no life can exist without it. It is the chemistry of life itself—shaping, defining, and sustaining our natural world. These projects will help you explore both its physical and chemical constituents and the way they impact our environment.

A CLOSER LOOK AT

Fast Waters—Springs, Streams, and Creeks

Fast waters offer a unique opportunity to examine the interrelationships of the physical, chemical, and biological factors that shape these dynamic communities:

The speed of a body of water determines what type of food is present and what feeding strategies organisms use.

The pH level affects life-forms. The higher the pH, the more carbonates, bicarbonates, and salts are present. These chemical constituents make water nutritionally rich and capable of supporting abundant microlife. When the pH is below 5 or above 10, the environment is hostile to most life-forms.

The type of riverbed greatly influences the diversity of life as well as the production of minerals in fast waters. Sandy bottoms and bedrock are the least productive, as they offer little protection or sites for attachment. Gravel, rocks, and rubble support the most diversity and are therefore the most productive habitats in fast water environments.

Visit a shallow creek or stream near you and do some of these projects to explore the world of fast waters. Use Figure 4-1 as a guide.

• Mark off 100 feet with stakes along the length of the stream. Draw an outline map of the stream in your field notebook; show the scale and indicate which direction is north. Make your map as detailed as possible, including both natural and man-made features: trees, islands, dams, swampy ground, roads, hillsides, and buildings. Make a *transect* at three places along the 100-foot section: Suspend a string across the width of the stream and secure its end at each side.

• Find the average depth of the stream within the 100-foot section. Wade into the stream and measure its depth at the three transects. Divide the total of the three depth measurements by 3 to get the average stream depth.

• Find out how fast the water is moving. Throw a stick 2 or 3 inches long into the water above the upstream 100-foot marker. Record the number of seconds it takes to float between the markers. Perform the following calculation:

100 feet ÷ Time (seconds) = Speed of stick (Feet per second)

• Find the average width of a section of the stream. Use a tape measure to measure the width of the stream at the three transects. Divide the total of the three measurements by 3 to get the average width of the stream.

• To find the flow volume, multiply the average width times average depth times the number of feet the stick floated each second. This will tell you the number of cubic feet of water flowing in the stream every second.

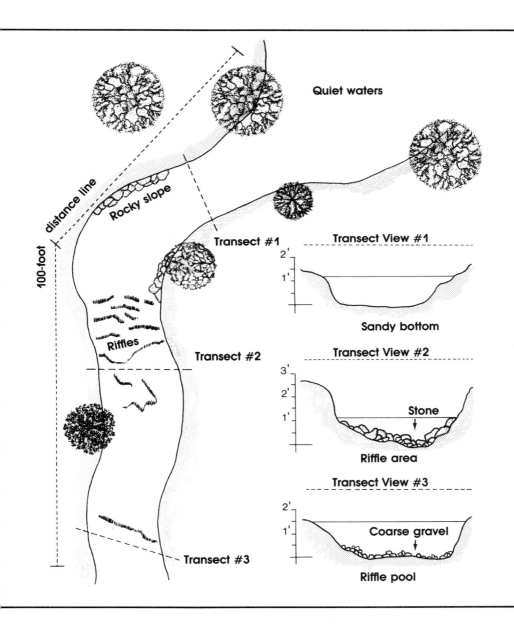

Figure 4-1   Investigating Fast Waters

$$\begin{matrix} \text{Average} \\ \text{width} \end{matrix} \times \begin{matrix} \text{Average} \\ \text{depth} \end{matrix} \times \text{Feet/sec} = \begin{matrix} \text{Cubic ft. of water} \\ \text{flowing per sec.} \end{matrix}$$

• Construct a bottom profile of the stream. At several intervals along each transect, measure water depth and classify type of bottom material (sand, gravel, stone, etc.) and amount and kind of vegetation (green microlife coatings or submerged vegetation as illustrated in Figure 4-4). Use a suitable scale to draw a cross-sectional profile of your stream.

• In your field notebook, record the clarity of the water along the 100-foot marked distance by direct observation or by using a secchi disc (see p. 79).

• Measure the pH (see p. 81) of samples taken at various locations. Do values differ?

• Use reference books to identify the types of plants found along the bank or shore. Draw them in your notebook. Research why these types of plants are usually found near water areas and not anywhere else.

• Use Figure 4-2 as a guide in making a stream bottom sampler or "kick net" to collect organisms trapped in bottom sediments. Stake the net downstream of where you plan to sample. Use a stick to lightly disturb sediments directly in front of the net's opening. When sampling along a transect, reposition the net along the string. Examine your collection in a white pan or tray. Use a magnifying glass and forceps when examining specimens. Refer to Figure 4-3 or other reference sources at the end of this chapter to help you identify them.

• Use a plankton net (see Figure 4-2) to sample plankton. Simply stake out the net in the middle of the stream and leave it there for 1-2 hours. Retrieve and study the collected life-forms under a microscope. Use field guides and a stereomicroscope to identify them.

• Use the preceding methods to learn how climatic events affect the stream. For example, how does storm water runoff from a heavy (or light) rain affect stream velocity hours or days after its occurrence? Gather data on other streams or creeks and compare them.

SECCHI DISK

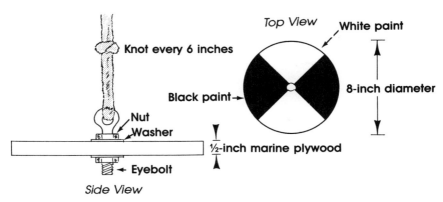

KICK NET

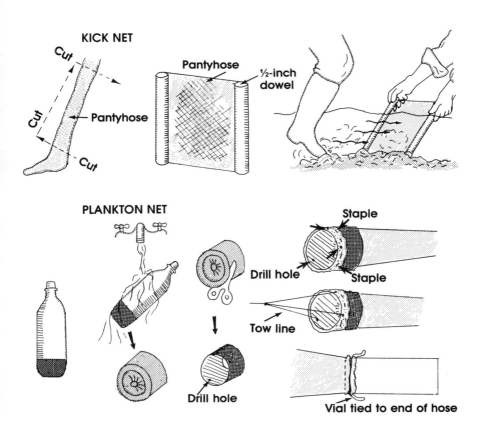

PLANKTON NET

Figure 4-2   Stream Sampling Techniques

• Investigate how *siltation* can damage habitats. Siltation occurs when soil particles wash downstream and accumulate after a heavy rain or because of poor agricultural or careless construction practices.

HOW SMALL IS SMALL?

Investigating Water Pollutants

You may have heard the terms *parts per million* or *parts per billion* used to describe water quality. They sound intimidating, but they merely express the concentration of a pollutant in the water. This project will help you better understand the meaning of the terms *concentration* and *dilution* and how they are expressed. You will also learn to test for the presence of a pollutant you cannot see!

What you need:

white vinegar
red food coloring
2 glasses of water
medicine dropper
10 plastic pop bottle screw-caps
pH test strips (see Making Your Own
   pH Paper on p. 82)
box of toothpicks

What to do:

First simulate a pollutant by mixing red food coloring and vinegar.

1. On a table, arrange nine bottle caps in a line and number them from 1 to 9.

2. In the tenth cap, combine five drops of red coloring with five drops of white vinegar; mix with a clean toothpick. This mixture is the simulated toxic chemical (STC).

3. Use the other glass of water for diluting your STC. In cap 1, combine one drop of STC with nine drops of water; mix with a clean toothpick. The concentration of STC is 1 part (STC) per 10 total parts, which is equivalent to 100,000 parts per million (ppm).

4. Transfer one drop of the polluted water mixture from cap 1 to cap 2. Add nine drops of water and mix with a new toothpick. Now the STC concentration is $\frac{1}{10}$ of $\frac{1}{10}$, or 10,000 ppm.

5. Transfer one drop of the polluted water from cap 2 to cap 3. Add nine drops of water and mix with a new toothpick. The STC concentration is $\frac{1}{10}$ of $\frac{1}{10}$ of $\frac{1}{10}$, or 1,000 ppm.

6. Duplicate Step 5, continuing to progressively dilute the STC from cap 4 to cap 9. Calculate the resulting concentrations of the STC in these caps.

Analyzing your data:

• At what concentration can the red color of the STC still be observed?
• In many instances, environmental scientists cannot detect a pollutant by seeing it: they rely on specific tests to determine its presence and concentration. Use pH paper to detect the presence of the STC in caps that show no visible evidence. What conclusions can you draw about potential chemical releases to the environment?

WHAT'S THE pH?

Acidity is expressed by pH, which is a logarithmic number. Thus, a one-unit change in pH is actually a 10-fold change in acidity— the concentration of hydrogen ions (H^+) in a solution. For example, pure distilled water has a pH of 7.0, which is called neutrality; the pH scale runs from 0 to 14 units. A solution that has a pH of 6.0 is 10 times more acidic (contains 10 times more H^+) than pure water, and a solution whose pH is 5.0 is 100 times more acidic than pure water.

MAKING YOUR OWN pH PAPER

The pH is measured by using indicators—substances that change color in response to various pH levels. Litmus, a blue powder extracted from lichens, is commonly used in litmus paper, which measures pH. You can make your own indicator paper using other plant pigments called anthocyanins, whose colors range from rich reds to dark blues, depending on the acidity of the solution.

What you need:

red cabbage
sauce pan
knife and chopping board
sheets of 100 percent rag paper
mason jar and lid
strainer
clothespins and suspended clothesline
7 soda bottle caps
white vinegar, lemon, magnesium hydroxide
    (milk of magnesia), household ammonia solution

What to do:

1. Under adult supervision, chop the cabbage into small pieces and place in a saucepan. Cover the cabbage with water. Heat until it almost boils, stirring the liquid until a deep red color is obtained. Allow to cool.

2. Carefully pour the mixture through a strainer into a mason jar to separate the cabbage pieces from the liquid anthocyanin extract. Discard the cabbage material.

3. Cut 100 percent rag paper (available at stationery stores) into 1- by 8-inch strips. Immerse the paper strips into the anthocyanin extract; then remove the strips, hang them up with clothespins, and allow them to dry.

***Caution:* Put on protective eyewear.**

• Dissolve a few grains of baking soda in water in a plastic bottle cap. Pour small amounts of the following materials into separate plastic bottle caps: white vinegar, lemon squeezings, tap water, solution of magnesium hydroxide (milk of magnesia), household ammonia.

— Dip 1-inch-square pieces of your anthocyanin paper into each solution. Allow the paper to dry. In your notebook, record the color change for each solution as well as the pH value from the following table:

Lemon juice	2.4 pH unit
Vinegar	3.0 pH unit
Pure water	7.0 pH unit
Milk of magnesia	10.0 pH unit
Ammonia solution	11.0 pH unit

— In your notebook, create a color chart by arranging previously dipped indicator paper along a horizontal axis in ascending pH units, from 0 to 14. This color chart will serve as your pH standard.

• Repeat the previous tests with litmus paper and compare the results to the anthocyanin results. How accurate is the chart?

OTHER pH PROJECTS

• Use your anthocyanin paper to test other common substances around the home including rain and melted snow. See the next project.

• Find out whether anthocyanins are present in other plant materials, such as turnips, beets, rose petals, and others.

ACID RAIN

Acid rain is a popular term that refers to rain, snow, or other precipitation contaminated by acids. It forms when water vapor in the air reacts with certain chemical compounds (nitrogen oxides and sulfur dioxides) from industrial, automotive, and power-generating sources. Environmental scientists use *acid deposition* to refer to both wet and dry acid pollution that falls to Earth.

What we call "acid rain" is any rain with a pH below 5.6. Most organisms can live within only a narrow pH range in their environment: a pH change of 1 or 2 units can eliminate a great number of plants and animals in an aquatic system. In acid lakes, where a variety of aquatic life once flourished, simpler plants and algae now exist. Also, dead leaves and twigs can become pickled in acid water; that means they don't decompose and release nutrients back into the environment.

The change in pH also affects the chemical composition of the water. Many substances normally found in minute quantities reach high concentrations in acid lakes. Try some of these projects:

• Collect rainwater in cleaned containers at various times during a rainstorm or snowstorm. Use litmus paper or anthocyanin paper (see the previous project) to measure the pH. If possible, compare data with friends in other cities that experience acid deposition.

• Collect water samples from different lakes, ponds, or streams near you. Measure the pH and compare these values to the pH of commercial household products.

• Vinegar preserves food like pickles and sauerkraut because its acidity inhibits decomposition. Some lakes are as acidic as vinegar! Place leaves (and other fruits or vegetables) in white vinegar and use a camera or video camera to record what happens over 4 to 6 weeks. Set up a control with the same items using water instead of vinegar.

• Each year air pollutants cause millions of dollars of damage to plants, buildings, statuaries, and stained glass. Marble is a form of calcium carbonate (calcite), a major building component. Obtain a small flake of white marble (ask the owner of a gravestone-monument or a landscaping company for a small piece). *Never alter or remove any material from headstones in cemeteries or buildings.* Wear protective eye goggles. Place a small flake in a paper cup and add a small amount of white vinegar, which is 5 to 7 percent acetic acid. Use a magnifying glass to examine the reaction. What effect does this acidified solution have on marble? What is the gas being given off? If you live in or near a city in the East, can you see evidence of air pollution on buildings or statuaries?

For advanced young scientists

SURVIVAL OF AQUATIC
ORGANISMS IN ACIDIC ENVIRONMENTS

Aquatic animals have varying sensitivity to acid in their habitats. This project explores how zooplankton react to acidification.

What you need:

zooplankton net (see Figure 4-2 to make your own)
2 mason jars
pH paper
white vinegar
medicine dropper
1-ounce measuring cup

What to do:

1. Use a plankton net (see p. 79) to collect a variety of aquatic microlife-forms from a nearby pond. Also collect samples of pond or lake water as well as a jar of bottom sediments.

2. Create a miniature pond or lake ecosystem by placing a small layer of bottom sediments (no more than ½ inch) into a mason jar. Add the collected water and aquatic plants. Place your pond/lake ecosystem near a window so that it will receive indirect (northern) sunlight.

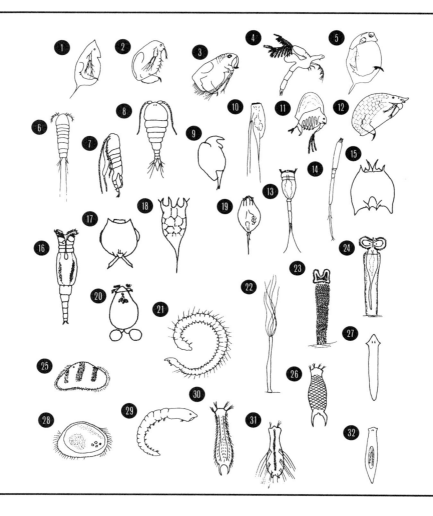

Figure 4-3   Visual Guide to Aquatic Organisms

Cladocerans, such as water fleas, are found in quiet waters. They include: (1) *Daphnia galeata*, (2) *Macrothrix*, (3) *Acantholeberis*, (4) *Leptodora*, (5) *Daphnia magna*, (11) *Holopedium*, (12) *Graptoleberis*. Copepods, also found in quiet waters, include: (6) *Canthocamptus*, (7) *Diaptomus*,

3. Place approximately 25 each of various large zooplankton forms (use Figure 4-3 as a guide in identification)—*Daphnia,* copepods, ostracods, amphipods—into your miniature pond/ lake ecosystem. Record in your notebook which zooplankton forms were added as well as the pH of the collected water.

4. Prepare a "control" system—an identical mason jar containing only an equal volume of collected water.

5. To each jar, slowly add 1 ounce (30 ml) of vinegar—drop by drop—using a medicine dropper. Use litmus or anthocyanin paper to measure the pH in both jars. Record the pH values in your notebook. Add acid each day for 1 week or until the pH reaches 3.8, which is the pH of most acid lakes. Record any deaths.

---

(8) *Mesocyclops.* Rotifers, found among aquatic vegetation and in bottom sediments, include: (9) *Colurella,* (10) *Filinia,* (13) *Scaridium,* (14) *Rotaria,* (15) *Branchionus,* (16) *Philodina,* (17) *Lecane,* (18) *Keratella,* (19) *Trichocera,* (20) *Pompholyx,* (23) *Floscularia,* (24) *Limnias.* Ostracods are found on green protists and among decaying vegetation: (25) *Cypridopsis,* (28) *Cyclocypris.* Hydroids are found attached to plants in quiet waters: (22) *Hydra.* Planarians live at the edge of ponds under submerged leaves and under rocks in quiet waters: (27) *Dugesia,* (32) *Phagocata.* Microannelids, found in bottom sediments, include: (21) *Dero,* (29) *Chaetogaster.* Gastrotrichs live on aquatic vegetation and within bottom sediments: (26) *Lepidodermella,* (30) *Chaetonotus,* (31) *Stylochaeta.*

Analyzing your data:
  • Did the pH fall (did the acidity increase), in equal increments for both containers after the daily addition of vinegar? If
not, design an additional experiment to identify the cause. HINT:
In many cases, sediments contain dissolved substances that act
as *buffers,* "chemical sponges" able to "soak up" added acids
or bases so that the pH of a solution is little affected.
  • Did certain organisms survive better than others? Which
organisms are most sensitive to acidity?

THE MYSTERY OF PARADOX LAKE

In New York State, almost all the lakes in the Adirondacks are
acidified—except Paradox Lake. Try this project to determine
why.
  Create two models of Adirondack lakes by filling two glasses,
each with 2 ounces (60 ml) of distilled or bottled water. Place
five antacid tablets (available at drugstores) in the bottom of
one glass and allow them to dissolve, undisturbed overnight. The
next day, gently swirl the mixture to dissolve as much material as
possible. A white residue will remain on the bottom. Record the
initial pH of both "lakes" in your field notebook. Record the pH
of a small amount of white vinegar. Carefully add a single drop
of white vinegar to each lake; swirl to mix and record the pH.
Repeat this procedure for each of nine more drops (ten total).
These drops simulate acid rain runoff into both lakes. Plot the pH
against the number of drops added. Is one lake more "stable"
than the other? What is the material responsible? Which model
represents Paradox Lake? Research why this lake deserves its
curious name.

For advanced young scientists

FERTILIZERS AND
SURFACE WATER RUNOFF

One of the many effects of pollution on aquatic environments
is the growth of microlife forms. For example, high levels of phos-

phates and nitrates, chemical compounds extensively used in fertilizers, in watershed runoff can cause explosive growth of microlife in lakes and ponds. In some cases microlife growth can be so dense as to stain wooden oars green! Such growth robs water of oxygen and can kill fish in massive numbers. The table below gives a small sampling of other environmental problems caused by the explosive growth of specific microlife forms.

Microorganism	Type	Problem
Anacystis	Cyanobacterium	Produces organic sulfur compounds and sulfur odor
Oscillatoria	Cyanobacterium	Produces geosmin, a substance that causes "earthy odors"
Pandorina	Green protist	Gives the water a "fishy" odor
Euglena	Green protist	Most pollution-tolerant microlife form. One species, E. rubra, is believed to have turned the river red as described in Exodus 7:20–21

You will see how fertilizers affect aquatic life in the following experiment.

What you will need:

3 mason jars; 2 lids
fertilizer (containing phosphates)
1-ounce measuring cup
dried and chopped grass clippings
pipettes and a compound microscope

What to do:

1. Go to a local pond, ditch, or similar water body and fill two mason jars two-thirds full of water. Designate one jar as the "control," the other as "experimental."

2. Fill the third mason jar two-thirds full of water. Add 1 tablespoon of fertilizer and mix. Label the jar "runoff."

3. To each jar, add a small amount of dried, chopped grass clippings.

4. Loosely cover each jar with lids and place them on a windowsill that receives indirect sunlight.

5. Add approximately 2 tablespoons of "runoff" solution from the third jar to the "experimental" jar every 2 days. Mix.

Analyzing data:

• Record in your notebook the exact chemical makeup of the fertilizer you used. Analyze this "runoff" solution by testing it with a soil test kit (available at a local garden center) and record how much phosphate and other chemical constituents are being added to your "experimental" container.

• At the beginning of the experiment use a pipette to sample the experimental and control jars and prepare wet mounts (see Chapter 2) for examination under a compound microscope. Use Figure 2-4 as a guide in identifying microlife forms. Record both the names of the microorganism and an estimate of each organism's abundance.

• Calculate the Biodiversity Index (see Chapter 2) for this water sample. In your calculations, use an average of 10 microscope fields at X120 to arrive at taxon numbers.

• Sample each jar at regular intervals. Identify and record the kind and number of microlife forms present. Calculate and compare the Diversity Index of the two jars—"control" versus "experimental."

• Continue sampling over as long a period as possible—at least 1 month. Over this period do you notice a change in water color, kinds and numbers of microlife forms, presence of odors? Make sure to record all your data in your notebook.

OTHER PROJECTS
• Take a census near where you live to find out how many households apply lawn fertilizers. Calculate the average amount of fertilizer applied per unit area of lawn (use information on commercial products in local garden centers as a guide). How close is the relative concentration of applied commercial fertilizers to the concentration used in the above experiment?
• Use an oven baster to capture surface runoff (from streets where fertilizer application has been documented) following a rain. Use this water instead of the artificial "runoff" water, containing a known amount of fertilizer, in an additional experiment. Are the results the same?
• Fill mason jars two-thirds with runoff water from various sources (roads, ditches, or other impervious surfaces) or create an artificial sample by mixing 1 tablespoon of fertilizer with 1 quart of water. Use a soil test kit (available at local garden stores) to test for levels of phosphorus, and nitrates, and pH. Record the data in your field notebook. Collect duckweed (*Lemna*), a common floating aquatic plant (see Figure 4-4), and add it to each of the jars. Position the jars so that they receive southern light exposure or place them under an aquarium light. Sample the water after a period of 4 to 6 weeks to find out whether these tiny plants remove pollutants—phosphorus or nitrates.

A CLOSER LOOK AT

Quiet Waters—Marshes, Ditches, Ponds, and Lakes

Ponds and lakes are the repositories of fresh water. They are created and continuously fashioned in many ways. These relatively still waters offer striking contrasts to fast waters: the gradations of light, temperature, and oxygen have a much greater

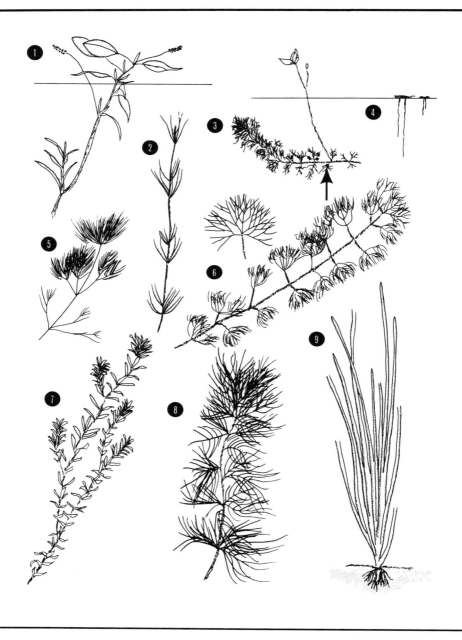

influence on the distribution and adaptations of life in lakes and ponds.

• Use Figure 4-2 as a guide to constructing a Secchi disk, an instrument that helps you estimate the depth of light penetration into a body of water. Take a metal disk about 8 inches in diameter and paint it with several coats of white enamel paint. Then divide the disk into quadrants and paint alternate sectors red or black. Attach the disc by a center rod to a length of chain or rope marked with distance from the disk every 6 to 12 inches. To obtain a reading, lower the disk over the side of a boat or pier and note the depth at which it seems to disappear. Sink the disk several more feet, then raise it, noting the depth at which it reappears. The average of these two observations gives a single light-penetration reading. Use the Secchi disk to determine whether aquatic plants grow below light-penetration levels.

• Draw a map of a pond or small lake near where you live. Include major zones of vegetation—around its perimeter as well as at the bottom. Use Figure 4-4 and references at the end of this chapter to help you indentify the plants; record your findings, including drawings of identified forms, in your notebook. If possible, use a boat to conduct transects, making depth soundings to construct a depth profile map as in Figure 4-5; take soundings with a weighted, marked line.

Figure 4-4   Visual Guide to Aquatic Plants

(1) Variable pondweed (*Potamogeton gramineus*) is found inland in fresh water and usually has floating leaves (2) Muckgrass (*Chara*) has a "skunky" odor and is often coated with lime.
(3) Eastern bladderwort (*Utricularia gibba*) is buoyed by tiny air bladders (see arrow).
(4) Duckweed (*Lemna*) forms a green blanket on quiet waters. (5) *Nitella* is bluish-green. (6) Fanwort (*Cabomba caroliniana*), (7) common elodea (*Elodea canadensis*), (8) whorled watermilfoil (*Myriophyllum verticillatum*), and (9) wild celery (*Vallisneria americana*) are all found inland in fresh water.

• Tow a plankton net (see Figure 4-2) at various depths—at the surface, 1 meter, 3 meters—to determine the organism count as well as the Diversity Index (see Chapter 2) of the pond or lake.

• Examine stones, leaves, and stems of floating and rooted plants for microlife. Note the life-forms characteristic of the following habitats: soil between the roots and stems of emergent plants, the underside of floating leaves, the surface of stems, submerged plants.

• Use a shovel to sample pond sediments, examine them in a white-colored pan or tray. Use Figure 4-3 as a guide in identifying sediment creatures.

For advanced young scientists

BIOLOGICAL INDICATORS OF POLLUTION

After years of research, the environmental scientist C. Mervin Palmer concluded in 1969 that the presence of certain microlife forms in aquatic habitats is a strong indicator of pollution.

In this project you will use his *Palmer Index* to find the level of pollution in water bodies near where you live. Follow Figure 4-6 to guide you through the procedure.

What you need:

compound microscope (magnification of X100)
microscope slides, coverslips (22 by 22 mm)
plankton net
iodine solution (Betadine)
beaker (1 liter); graduated cylinder (100 ml)
baby food jars
5 test tubes
pipettes

What to do:

1. Collect samples of river or lake waters with a plankton net (see p. 79).

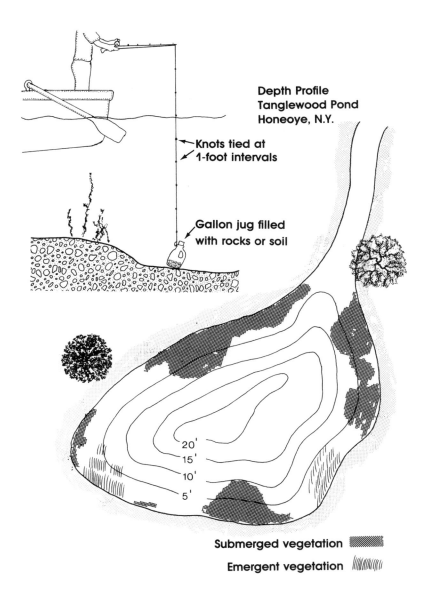

Depth Profile
Tanglewood Pond
Honeoye, N.Y.

Knots tied at
1-foot intervals

Gallon jug filled
with rocks or soil

20'
15'
10'
5'

Submerged vegetation
Emergent vegetation

Figure 4-5   Constructing a Depth Profile
Have a friend take down readings while you measure the
depth of a pond using a weighted jug at the end of a rope
or fishing line. You should be able to determine the depth by
counting the knots tied at 1-foot intervals. If possible, conduct
transects in a boat, making enough depth measurements to
construct a depth profile similar to the one shown.

2. *Caution:* **Wear protective eyewear for this step.** Mix the plankton sample, withdraw 10 ml with a pipette, and place in a test tube. Add one drop of iodine solution (Betadine) to kill all the cells. This subsample will be used to identify and count the microlife to arrive at the Palmer score.

3. Prepare a wet mount using a *single drop* taken with a clean pipette from the subsample.

4. Count the microlife in at least 4 different "strips" of the slide under a X100 microscope. The process of moving across the slide to get different fields of view is called a strip scan.

— Consider a colony and a single cell as equivalent units in your counting. Count large filaments and/or colonies that are partially in the field of view as fractions of a single unit. Figure 2-4 will help identify microlife forms.

Use the following formula to calculate the *organism density*—the number of organisms in a milliliter of the sample:

$$\text{Organism density} = \frac{[A] \times [B]}{[C] \times [D] \times [E]} \times 0.1 \, \frac{[484] \times [51]}{[44] \times [4] \times [0.1]}$$
$$= 140 \text{ organisms per liter}$$

where:

A = area of coverslip (22 x 22 mm = 484 mm²)
B = number of microlife forms counted (51)
C = area of strip (2 x 22 mm = 44 mm²)
D = number of strips scans counted (4)
E = volume of subsample under coverslip (0.1 ml)
0.1 = conversion factor

— For example, say a four-strip scan of the sample found 51 *Chlamydomonas* cells. The calculation would reveal a total organism density of 140 *Chlamydomonas* cells per milliliter of water. To receive a Palmer score, a group of like organisms (a taxon) must have a density of at least 50. In our example then, Chlamydomonas would receive a Palmer Score of 4 on the basis of the following table:

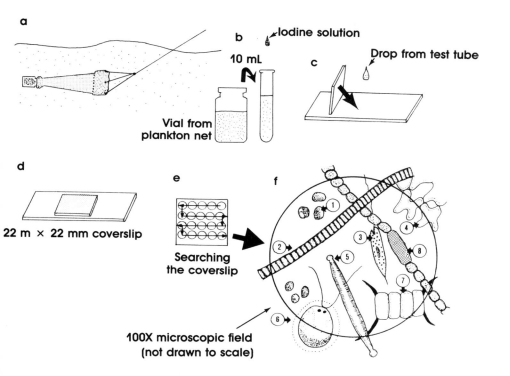

a

b Iodine solution

10 mL

Vial from plankton net

c Drop from test tube

d

22 m × 22 mm coverslip

e

Searching the coverslip

f

100X microscopic field
(not drawn to scale)

Figure 4-6   Counting Microlife to Determine Pollution Levels
(a) Collect microorganisms with a plankton net in open water.
(b) Place 10 mL of your sample in a test tube; add 1 drop of
iodine solution to kill cells. (c) Place 1 drop from the test tube
onto a microscope slide. (d) Place a coverslip over the drop.
(e) Examine the slide with a 100X microscope, counting the
microlife in each field of view. Move across the slide systematically in rows as shown. (f) This is what a typical microscopic
field would look like. Count a life-form that appears only
partially within the field of view as a whole organism. For this
field, you would count a *Chlorella* (1), an *Oscillatoria* (2), a
Euglena (3), a *Pediastrum* (4), a *Synedra* (5), a *Chlamydomonas* (6), a *Scenedesmus* (7), and an *Anabaena.* To
determine the pollution level, calculate the Palmer score
according to the directions on page 96.

Genus	Pollution Index Value	Genus	Pollution Index Value
Anacystis	1	*Micractinium*	1
Ankistrodesmus	2	*Navicula*	3
Chlamydomonas	4	*Nitzschia*	3
Chlorella	3	*Oscillatoria*	5
Closterium	1	*Pandorina*	1
Cyclotella	1	*Phacus*	1
Euglena	5	*Phormidium*	1
Gomphonema	1	*Scenedesmus*	4
Lepocinclis	1	*Stigeoclonium*	2
Melosira	1	*Synedra*	2

Source: Adapted from Palmer, *Journal of Phycology* 5:1 (1969), 78–82.

— A separate calculation must be made for each microlife form you count in the sample.

Analyzing your data:
The following table is a sample set of data:

June 25, 1993 Data for Tanglewood Pond

Number of Organisms	Genus	Palmer Index Value
59	*Melosira*	1
68	*Peridinium*	Δ
21	*Euglena*	†
98	*Synedra*	2
55	*Micractinium*	1
61	*Chlorella*	$\frac{3}{}$
	Total	7

Δ Not a microlife indicator.
† Insufficient number.

This composite Palmer score is then compared to the ranges in the following table to determine whether organic loading (pollution) is high, moderate, or low:

Composite Palmer Score	Indication
20+	High organic loading (pollution)
15–19	Moderate organic loading
<15	No or very low organic loading

With a composite Palmer score of 7, Tanglewood Pond is relatively pollution-free. It should be able to support a wide variety of aquatic life.

INVESTIGATING STORM WATER RUNOFF

The EPA has calculated that runoff from the first hour of a moderate to heavy storm in a typical U.S. city would contribute more pollution load to water bodies than the same amount of the city's untreated sewage during the same period. Urban and suburban runoff contain contaminants such as sediments, salt, phosphorus, nitrates, coliform bacteria, and lead and other heavy metals that can impair water quality in streams, lakes, wetlands, and estuaries.

Investigate the environmental impacts of storm water runoff in areas where you live by doing one or all of these projects:

INVESTIGATING THE EFFECTS OF STORM WATER ON PLANTS
After a rainfall, collect water samples with a kitchen baster from various sites (parking lots, city streets, paved urban/rural roads, etc.), and seal them in quart-capacity mason jars. Label the jar with the location, time of collection, and duration and amount of rainfall. Study the effect of watering bean seeds or other plants with collected runoff water versus distilled water as a control. For each sample, plant four to six seeds in a 4-inch pot. Record your observations of percentage germination, plant height, and color in your field notebook.

• Calculate how much untreated storm water passes directly into streams, rivers, and other water bodies after a rain without filtering through soils or wetlands. (Approximately 0.6 gallon [2,270 ml] drains off a square foot of impervious surface after 1 inch of heavy rain.)

ROAD SALTING

• In certain communities across the country, salts are applied to road surfaces to melt snow and ice. Road salts are compounds that raise the melting point of ice on contact to facilitate travel on cold, wintry days.

— Study how road salts melt ice by placing small amounts of commercially available deicing products containing either halite (sodium chloride), calcium chloride, or calcium magnesium acetate (CMA) on top of ice cubes at room temperature. Record your observations in your notebook. Which deicing material is the most efficient at melting ice at room temperature; at colder temperatures such as those inside a freezer compartment?

— Conduct "field trials" by applying different deicing materials to a walkway or driveway and observe their action at various temperatures. Is calcium chloride a better low-temperature deicer than rock salt? Determine what temperature range is best for applying road salt to remove ice.

• In geographic areas where road salt is effective, it is estimated that road crews apply 400 pounds of salt for every level two-lane mile (twice that on hills). Since road lanes are usually 11 feet in width, this translates to, on average, 1.5 grams of salt per square foot of road surface. The first inch of water (snow or rain) that falls on an impervious road surface will carry the salt away by sheet drainage. (About 2,300 ml, two-thirds gallon of water per square foot runs off impervious surfaces after 1 inch of precipitation.)

— Contact the public works department to find out how many paved two-lane miles exist in your town or county area and how often road salt is applied every winter. Calculate how much road salt is applied to county or town roads where you live.

— Calculate the concentration of salt washing off the road surface in a winter season—1.5 grams in 2,300 ml times the number of seasonal applications. Water grass and other plants with an equivalent concentration. How does it affect the plants? Can you observe similar effects along roadsides in the spring?

• In urban areas, storm sewers capture a large volume of this runoff and direct it to discharge points—usually rivers and streams—with little, if any, treatment prior to discharge. Pollutants, like road salt, are thus directly discharged into water bodies like lakes and ponds. To get a feeling for the extent of this impact over time on a lake or pond, try this project:

— Add 2 teaspoons of table salt (sodium chloride) to a glass of water, stir until all the salt dissolves. Add a drop of blue food coloring to the salt water. Fill a mason jar half-full with water. Slowly, pour the blue-colored salt water down the side of the mason jar so that it trickles into the jar. Observe what is happening. Continue your observations over the next couple of days.

Learn More About It

WATER RECREATION AREAS	For FREE maps write to: Department of the Army, Corps of Engineers, 2803 52nd Avenue, Hyattsville, MD 20781-1102
WILDLIFE REFUGES	For FREE map write to: U.S. Fish and Wildlife Service, Division of Refuge, 18th and C Streets NW, Washington, DC 20204
WETLANDS	For list of FREE publications, write: Department of the Interior, Fish and Wildlife Service, Publications Unit, Mail Stop: 130 Webb Building, 4401 North Fairfax Drive, Arlington, VA 22023

WETLANDS MAP OF	For FREE map illustrating all
UNITED STATES	federal wetlands, write: U.S. Fish &
	Wildlife Service, National
	Wetlands Inventory, ATTN: Map
	Distribution, 9720 Executive
	Center Dr., Suite 101, St.
	Petersburg, FL 33702

Read More About It

EPA *Water Pollution Aspects of Street, Surface Contaminants.* EPA-R2-72-081, Office of Research & Monitoring. Washington, DC, Nov. 1972, pp. 137.

Hotchkiss, Neil. *Marsh, Underwater, and Floating-leaved Plants of the United States and Canada.* New York: Dover, 1972

Margulis, Lynn, and Karlene Schwartz. *Five Kingdoms: An Illustrated Guide to the Phyla of Life on Earth.* 2nd ed. New York: Freeman, 1988.

Mohnen, Volker A. "The Challenge of Acid Rain." *Scientific American* 259, 2: (August 1, 1988), 30–38.

National Academy of Sciences. *Acid Deposition: Long-Term Trends.* Washington, D.C.: National Academy Press, 1986.

Needham, James G., and Paul R. Needham. *A Guide to the Study of Freshwater Biology.* San Francisco: Holden-Day, 1962.

Pawlick, Thomas. *A Killing Rain: The Global Threat of Acid Precipitation.* San Francisco: Sierra Club Books. 1986.

Pennak, Robert. *Fresh-Water Invertebrates of the United States.* 3rd ed. New York: Wiley, 1989.

Petrovic, Anthony Martin. "Home Lawns." In *Cornell Cooperative Extension Publication Bulletin* 185. Ithaca, N.Y.: Cornell University Press, 1982.

5

THE LAND

The land shapes and defines our physical world. Its features influence, and in instances dictate, which life forms prosper and which wither. It is, however, a fragile foundation that can be irrevocably altered by carelessness and neglect. Following are projects that will help you understand how the land is a resource that must be protected so that it can continue to sustain.

THE SHAPE OF THE LAND

Learning About Topographic Maps
A *topographic map* illustrates the shape and elevation of the land as well as other man-made features, such as roads, bridges, and mines. The most important element of the topographic map is the *contour line*, which connects points of the same elevation on the map. The following project helps you create a contour map of a large rock—just the thing you need to do to understand topographic maps better!

Wash off a large, irregularly shaped rock. Tape a plastic ruler to the inside of a large bucket and place the rock inside the bucket. Add water until the rock is submerged. Use a dipper cup to lower the water level in 1-inch increments until the bucket is empty. At each successive 1-inch drop, mark a line around the rock with a grease pencil.

Remove the rock, allow it to dry, and place it on a sheet of white paper. Look down onto the rock. Use a pencil to draw a contour map of the rock from the previously traced waterline marks. Be sure to label each contour line with its height in inches. Suppose the rock were a mountain; if each contour line represented a change of 20 feet, how tall would your mountain be?

• Obtain a topographic map (see Learn More About It) of an area near where you live. Contour lines are brown on a standard U.S. Geological Survey map. The *contour interval* is the difference in elevation between any two consecutive contour lines. Use the *Rules Governing Contour Lines*, which follow, as a guide when studying any contour map:

— Contour lines are endless lines that never cross one another, branch, or fork.

— Closely spaced lines represent steep slopes; widely spaced lines represent gentle slopes.

— Usually, every fifth contour line is represented by a heavier line and is marked to indicate elevation.

— The direction of increasing elevation is toward the center of the circles approximated by the contour lines.

— When crossing a valley, contour lines form a V or U shape that always points upward in elevation.

For advanced young scientists

CONSTRUCTING A
TOPOGRAPHICAL RELIEF MODEL

Construct a three-dimensional model of a landform based on your topographic map using Figure 5-1 as a guide.

What you need:

plywood sheet (12 by 24 by ¼ in)
wood pieces

modeling clay (one or several colors)
wooden peg
back marker
ruler
¼-inch drill bit; electric drill
6-penny nails

What to do:

1. Construct the wooden frame as shown in Figure 5-1. Drill a ¼-inch hole in the center of the crosspiece rod as illustrated.

2. With a marker and ruler, divide the sides of the frame into the same number of divisions as the map and number them in the same manner. Divide the crosspiece rod into the same lettered divisions as the map, but mark the letters in reverse order. Place the rod over the frame. Make a stylus or peg that can move up and down in the hole in the rod. The stylus must be graduated according to the contour interval on the map, so make sure it is large enough to be numbered.

3. Begin with the highest land contour illustrated on the map. Position the rod at the coordinates on the map and let the stylus drop to the contour height. Then build clay up to the point of the stylus. Reposition the stylus to other coordinates and build clay to the indicated contour height. Model the remainder of the topography by hand with wood or wire sculpture tools from an art supply store.

WHAT'S THE SLOPE?

The contours of the land are expressed as percentage inclination—the *slope.* This important land feature often determines land-use practices. For example, slopes of 15 percent (or greater) are often designated "Limited Development Districts" and are protected from commercial development. Steep slopes that suffer loss of vegetative cover during construction are often

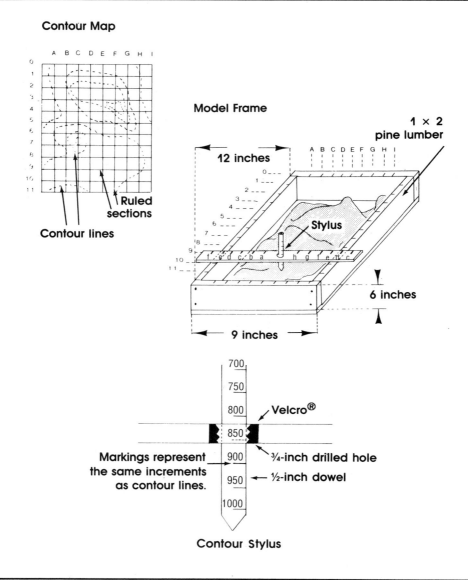

Figure 5-1   Constructing a Topographic Relief Model
From a contour map, build a model of the area's topography.

swiftly eroded because rapidly flowing water can carry away soil particles normally held by root systems.

You can measure the steepness of slopes by using some simple materials: a yardstick, a straight piece of wood exactly 50 inches long, and a carpenter's level or a flat-sided bottle that is half full of a colored liquid.

• In the field, lay the 50-inch wood piece on the ground along the slope you want to measure. Place the carpenter's level (or the bottle) on the wood piece and set the yardstick upright, at right angles to the wood piece. Carefully raise the wood piece with the carpenter's level until it is level.

• Read on the yardstick the distance from the ground to the bottom of the 50-inch wood piece. This reading in inches, multiplied by 2, gives the percentage slope.

• Compare and contrast erosion severity and slope percentage on slopes that have lost vegetative cover. Take photographs of field conditions to include in your notebook along with your calculations.

LEARN YOUR LDDs!

Find areas of steep slope on your topographic map by taking the following steps.

• Locate the map scale, which is usually in English units, and determine how many feet are represented by either a ½- or a 1-inch ruler increment. Carefully tape a piece of clear acetate over the section of the contour map you wish to study. Locate contour lines that indicate steep-slope areas. Measure either a ½- or a 1-inch distance at right angles to the contour lines and determine the difference in elevation in feet within this distance. Divide the difference in elevation by the distance in feet represented by the ruler increment. Multiply this value by 100 to obtain the percent slope. (For example, if a difference of 150 feet is measured [by counting contour lines] over a 1,000-foot map scale distance, the slope is 15 percent.)

• With a marker, shade in all areas on the overlay that meet the following characteristics: slopes greater than 15 percent, water areas, wetlands.

• Visit your town hall and find out whether zoning laws for LDDs are in effect in these areas. LDDs are sometimes called Environmental Protection Overlay Districts.

DETERMINING MAP AREAS

Use the grid and table in Figure 5-2 to calculate map areas. Obtain aerial photographs or topographic maps and determine the percentage of land in each of these categories: agricultural, open space (parks), urban development, industrial development, limited development district, wetlands.

WHAT FILLS THE PUDDLE

Studying Watersheds

The entire land area that supplies surface water runoff to fill anything from a single puddle to a large inland lake, wetland, or river is called its *watershed*. Watersheds are distinct geographic regions where water drains into a particular stream, into a wetland, and on into a river—and ultimately to the sea. River basin is a synonym for watershed. Watersheds are dominant features of the Earth's surface, ranging in size from small areas feeding streams to the basin of the Amazon River, covering an area twice the size of India.

• Use topographic or other maps (available at large stationery stores) or aerial photographs (see Learn More About It) of your region to trace local streams or rivers from their source to rivers that flow to the coast. Find out whether your community is located near:

Headwaters—very steep, small streams fed by rain, snow, glaciers, or springs. Water flows rapidly.

Middle Waters—water flowing slowly through comparatively flat land. They are often surrounded by a floodplain, which is inundated after a heavy rain or snow. Marshes and lakes are often along or near the river.

Mouth—fresh water mixes with salt water as the river courses out to sea. Currents are very slow.

• Use a marker to define your watershed area. Select a

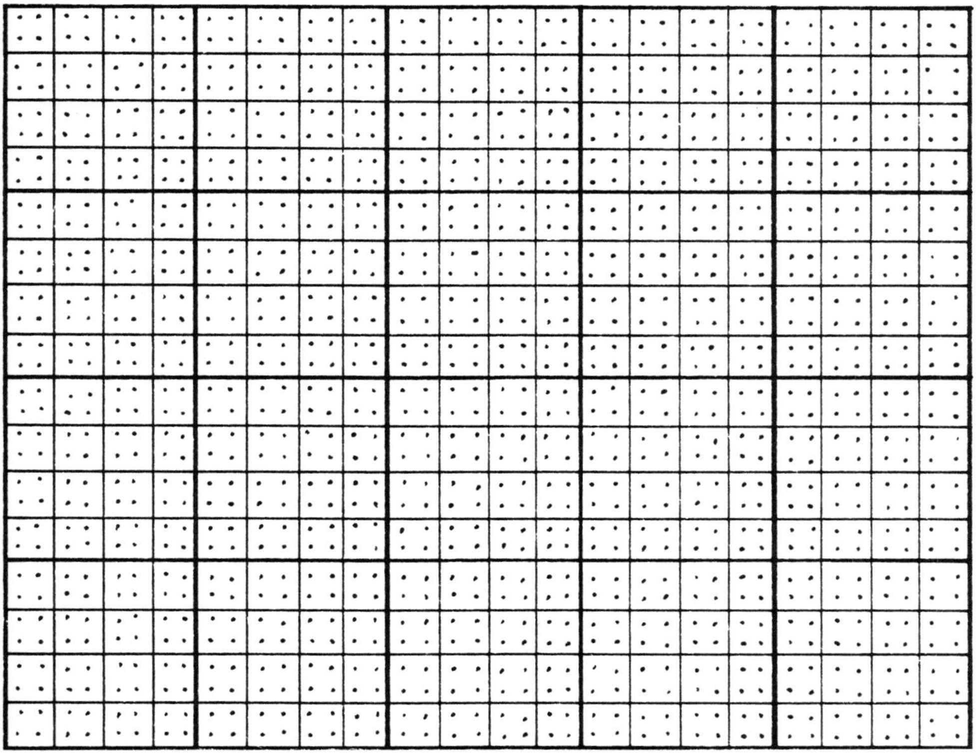

Figure 5-2 Determining Area on a Map or Aerial Photograph

Photocopy this page onto an acetate sheet. Randomly place the grid over an area of a topographic map or photograph of known scale to compute the area's acreage. Count the dots falling within the area (count every other dot on a boundary). Multiply by the conversion factor listed in the table to determine the acreage.

Scale	Area per square inch	Conversion (one dot equals)
1 inch: 500 feet	5.7 acres	0.089 acre
1 inch: 1,000 feet	22.9 acres	0.35 acre
1 inch: 200 feet	91.8 acres	1.43 acres
1 inch: 5,280 feet	640.0 acres	10.0 acres

portion of your watershed and analyze how human activity and pollutants affect environmental quality. Construct a simple map of your watershed and identify the following: population centers (both towns and cities), industrial areas, and agricultural uses.

SOIL

The Forgotten Resource

Soil is a complex mixture of inorganic minerals—clay, silt, pebbles, and sand—decaying organic matter, water, air, and living organisms. It is the biosphere in miniature, host to a complex web of interconnected processes that renew and recycle. Like fossil fuels, it is nonrenewable, and its production takes a very long time! The Department of Agriculture estimates that about *6 billion tons* of soil from farmlands and development practices is lost to erosion each year! That's enough to cover the state of Rhode Island 1 foot deep! Here are some projects that will better help you understand just what a precious resource soil is.

WHAT'S ON THE HORIZON?

Every soil has a history that affects its vulnerability to erosion. Soil forms through weathering and other processes that act on *parent material*—bedrock or other geologic material. Nearly all soils develop a series of different *horizons* or layers. In most undisturbed soil, the major horizons are called the surface, or *topsoil*, the *subsoil*, and the underlying *parent material*. Topsoil almost always has the highest organic content; subsoil has very low concentrations, and there is almost none in parent material.

• Locate and study soil horizons near where you live—in an eroded roadbank, a trench dug during construction, or a hole dug with a spade having a smooth, straight face. Use a yardstick to measure each layer. Sketch horizons studied in your field notebook. Be sure to include a scale so that you can compare horizon depths from various study locations.

SOIL PARTICLES ARE NOT CREATED EQUAL

The size of soil particles is important. The amount of interstitial space, the space between soil particles, determines how fast water moves through soil or how much water soil will hold. The Wentworth Scale (see table on the next page) details the relative progression of particle size and particle type. *Loam* refers to soils that have a favorable proportion of sand, silt, and clay—usually in equal amounts.

• Conduct a soil stratification test by filling a mason jar about two-thirds with water. Pour in dry soil until the jar is almost full. Replace the cover and shake the jar vigorously. Place the jar on a table and let the soil settle, allowing plenty of time (overnight) for the finest particles (clays) to settle. Hold a white index card against the side of the jar and draw a diagram of the various layers. Label each layer of clay, silt, or sand according to the descriptive terminology used in the Wentworth Scale. Also record the relative percentages of clay, silt, and sand in each sample.

• Sample other soils in the same manner from the area where you live. Compare and contrast your results in your field notebook. Try to obtain samples that illustrate as many Wentworth Scale types as possible as well as various combinations of clay, silt, and sand.

HOW FAST DOES IT PERK?

Percolation is the movement of water through soil. Percolation tests or perk tests are usually made to determine whether soils are suitable for septic systems. Good *infiltration*, the movement of water from the surface down to subsoils, is the hallmark of a good "perk" test result. Soils are classified in four water infiltration groups designated by letters as follows:

Group A   Sands/gravels: soils with high infiltration rates.

Group B   Fine to moderate textures (sandy loam): soils with moderate infiltration rates.

Group C   Clay loams, sandy soils high in clay; soils moderately fine in texture: soils with slow infiltration rates.

Group D   Clays: soils with very slow infiltration rates.

Wentworth Scale

Particle Size (mm)	Particle Type
>4	Pebble, cobble, boulder
4–2	Granule
2–1	Very coarse sand
1–0.5	Coarse sand
0.5–0.25	Medium sand
0.25–0.125	Fine sand
0.125–0.0625	Very fine sand
0.0625–0.004	Silt
<0.004	Clay

• Conduct perk tests at various places near where you live. Be sure to have permission before digging any holes. Use a trowel or spade to dig a hole approximately 12 inches deep and 6 inches in diameter. Fill the hole with water (a plastic milk jug is a handy carrier). In your field notebook record the time in minutes and seconds it takes for all the water to disappear into the soil. Set up a table that compares perk rate to hydrologic soil group. Refill the hole before leaving the area. Do wet or moist soils perk well?

GROUND COVER

The First Line of Defense Against Soil Erosion

Living plants, plant residue (mulch), and bits of rock on the surface of the soil intercept falling raindrops, thus preventing some erosion. Vegetative ground cover also slows the flow of water across the surface and increases the rate at which water infiltrates the soil.

• Study the erosion energy of raindrops by constructing splash boards that measure how far soil travels. Obtain pine boards 1 inch thick, 4 inches wide, and 3½ feet long. Sharpen one end of each board to a V-shape. Paint them white. Mark lines across the boards at 1-foot intervals beginning at the unsharpened end. Attach a 4-inch-square piece of galvanized metal to the flat end of each board to prevent rain from washing off splashed soil.

— Position the splash boards on bare ground—along a path in a school yard—and on a grassy spot with no exposed soil. Drive the sharpened end of each splash board into the ground to a depth of 6 inches. Leave them there and observe them after the first rain. (Or fill a sprinkling can and simulate rain by sprinkling the ground from a height of 3 to 5 feet.) Record the height of soil splashes. You may want to combine this project with making microdough balls (see Chapter 4) to study the size of raindrops and how much erosive energy they carry.

DEVISING STRATEGIES
TO PREVENT EROSION

For over 50 years farmers have been practicing soil conservation methods designed to minimize soil loss. Do the following projects to learn more about how crop cover, mulching, and contour plowing reduce soil erosion.

What you need:

5 shoe boxes lined with plastic sheeting
topsoil or garden soil
5 buckets
utility knife
wood blocks or similar supports
sprinkling can or a coffee can punched
   with small holes
sod pieces
garden mulch
pencil

What to do:

1. Use a utility knife to cut a V-shaped notch in an end of each shoe box that will function as a spout.

2. Fill box 1 with firmly packed, moist soil, box 2 with sod, box 3 with firmly packed moist soil covered with garden mulch, box 4 with packed moist soil with furrows running lengthwise made by a pencil, and box 5 with three strips of packed moist soil running crosswise alternating with three strips of sod.

3. Position the boxes on the same inclined support. Place buckets under the spouts to collect water and sediment runoff.

4. Sprinkle water steadily for 5 seconds onto each box. In your field notebook, record the amount of time the water continues to flow from the spout of each box. After the water has run off, measure the amount of sediment collected from each bucket.

• Which land practice(s) seem best for reducing soil erosion? Research other soil conservation practices and evaluate them similarly.

OTHER PROJECTS
• Simulate construction on steep slopes by making mounds of soil in the middle of two plastic-lined boxes or in two large round pie tins or dishpans. With a pencil or finger make furrows up and down the side of one mound and in circles around the other. Calculate the respective slopes for each mound. Sprinkle an equal amount of water over each mound and observe the water and soil runoff patterns created. Sketch these patterns in your notebook.
• If possible, visit some local areas that suffer from erosion, either natural or caused by poor land-management. Prepare a plan to repair the damage and prevent future loss of soil. You may want to use a camera or video camera for this work.

STUDYING A STREAM'S LOAD

The amount of material a stream carries at one time is its *load*. Streams transport these materials in one of three ways: in solution, suspension, and bed load. In the United States alone, it is estimated that streams carry nearly 300 tons of dissolved material, mainly minerals, to the seas each year. Multiply that by 4 billion years and you get an idea of why the oceans are salty.

THE INVISIBLE LOAD

The water picks up this invisible load as it courses over and through the land. Water is said to be hard or soft on the basis of the amount of dissolved salts (as magnesium and/or calcium carbonate) it contains.

• Hard water streams usually exhibit *primary production*, which means there is microlife growth and oxygen production because calcium and magnesium are so abundant in them. Soft water streams are just the opposite; they are nutrient-poor and have little primary production.

— Test for the presence of carbonates with a soil test kit (available at local garden centers). Make trips out into the field and sample various streams to determine whether they are hard or soft.

— Water hardness is the water's capacity to precipitate soap out of solution. The degree of hardness can be assessed by the amount of lather remaining after shaking a soapy solution for five minutes.

Conduct this test with two antacid tablets having either magnesium or calcium carbonate as the "active" ingredient. Dissolve them in a mason jar two-thirds full of water. (Crushing helps the tablets dissolve.) Fill another mason jar with a similar amount of water. Add a small, but equal, amount of soap (not detergent) to each jar. Agitate both jars for approximately 5 minutes. Compare the relative amounts of suds in both jars of water. The less the suds, the harder the water. Give water samples you've collected the "hardness shake test" and compare their hardness to the "antacid standard."

SUSPENDED SOLIDS

A stream's load is deposited when its velocity falls below the point necessary to hold suspended particles, such as when a stream empties into a larger body of water. If particle size is large enough, the load settles to the bottom as sediment.

• To investigate sediment deposition you will need a number of tall, narrow jars, such as olive jars, with caps. After a heavy rain, fill one of the jars from a small stream that gets at least part of its water from cultivated fields. Or fill it directly downstream from a construction project. Find another stream where all the water drains from woodlands and another from an established pasture or meadow. Use topographic maps, if necessary, to help determine drainage sources; try to capture water as close to the stream's middle as possible.

• Allow each of the water samples to settle for a few days. Observe them daily and record what you see in your field notebook. Which drainage conditions result in the least sedimentation; the most? If possible, trace the water course to find the point of erosion. Use a camera to record field conditions. Draw detailed maps to document field conditions fully.

BED LOAD

Particles too large (see Wentworth Scale) to be carried in suspension are instead bounced along the stream bottom with the ebb and flow of the stream's velocity. Such material is the stream's bed load.

• Sample streambeds to locate where bed loading occurs.

OTHER PROJECTS

• Using water velocity calculations you made in chapter 4, calculate the amount of sediment by volume, based on your field data, that your stream is carrying per hour. Take additional samples (every hour, if possible) to construct a sedimentation load profile for a given stream drainage during a 12- to 48-hour period after a heavy rain.

• If possible, trace the course of streams that empty into larger water bodies. Can you observe silt deposition?

INVESTIGATING LANDFILLS

Landfills are crucibles of containment, not of process. Today "garbologists," archaeologists who specialize in garbage containment areas, are unearthing disturbing surprises—biodegradable materials are not degrading! The following project lets you construct a miniature landfill and investigate how biodegradation processes are affected.

What you need:

6 transparent (8-ounce) plastic cups
thick, transparent plastic sheeting material
   (4 sheets, each 12 inches square)
moist (not wet) topsoil
spray bottle containing water
rubber bands
artist's brush
plastic sandwich bags
magnifying glass
landfill materials:
     — paper and plastic strips ($\frac{1}{2}$ x 2 inches)
     — cornstarch-based pellets (see Learn More About It)
     — "biodegradable plastic" material
     — synthetic and natural fiber material
     — dry leaves (chopped)
     — bread
     — grass clippings
     — strips of paper napkins saturated with red vegetable dye

What to do:

1. Label cups from 1 to 4.

2. Construct a state-of-the-art double-composite liner system. Place two sheets of plastic material inside cups 2 and 4. These cups simulate *sanitary* landfills, as opposed to nonlined or *open* landfills (cups 1 and 3).

3. Fill cups one-third full with topsoil.

4. Simulate a garbage bag ready for disposal by placing the following materials in a plastic sandwich bag: dyed paper, plastic strips, cornstarch pellets, synthetic or natural fiber, dry leaves, grass clippings, and bread. Fill two bags and seal them with cellophane tape. Make sure the sealed bags will fit comfortably within the plastic cup. Place sealed bags in cups 1 and 2.

5. Place additional *cover material* (topsoil) in cups 1 and 2—almost to the top of each cup.

6. Close these two landfills as follows: cup 1—establish *final cover* by adding soil to form a dome; *stabilize* slopes by planting grass; cup 2—gather the plastic sheets and use a rubber band to seal the liner system, add final cover, and stabilize.

7. Bury the same articles as in Step 4 in cups 3 and 4, but without the plastic "garbage bag." Position the materials so that their location can be viewed through the side of each cup. Close these landfills in the same way as cups 1 and 2.

8. Monitor your miniature landfills for 6 to 8 weeks—longer if possible. Record your observations in your field notebook. During this period, spray a gentle mist to simulate rain. Carefully monitor how rainwater infiltrates ground material. Take special note of any leachate—red dye carried by infiltrating water—migrating from the "contaminated" paper napkins.

9. *Caution:* **Wear protective gloves for this step.** After 8 weeks or longer carefully remove and examine each article in the landfill. With an artist's brush, carefully clean off the soil particles from each article.

Analyzing your data:
Examine the articles with a magnifying glass; look for differences in size, shape, texture; breaks in fibers, and fading of colors. Re-

cord your findings by material type in your field notebook, citing appearance, condition, color, and texture.

- Is the potential for leachate contamination greater with open landfills or sanitary landfills?
- Yard waste represents 15 to 20 percent of landfill volume; is there a better way to handle this waste stream?
- Can you determine how fast microbes break down materials for each landfilled item?
- Did you observe a foul, rotten egg smell when excavating your miniature landfills? What do you suspect is the cause? Is oxygen, or a lack of it, a significant factor?
- Did all materials degrade in the same manner? Are there similarities based on the type of material—cellulose fibers, starch molecules, plastics?
- On the basis of these observations, what can you conclude about biodegradation in sanitary and open landfills?
- Experiment with additional miniature landfills to determine whether other permeable materials—like sand or subsoils—are a better fill material.
- Research how municipal waste is handled in your community for each of these sources: industrial, household, and municipal (yard waste).
- Generally, 1 ton of material occupies 1 cubic yard of "air space" in a landfill. Roughly calculate how much landfill space your household consumes each year. Devise ways to save landfill space by changing your household routine.

Learn More About It

Watersheds/map area	FREE. An index of topographic maps by state by contacting: United States Geologic Survey (Department of the Interior) Branch of Distribution Box 25286, Federal Center, Denver, Colorado 80225 303/236-7477

Aerial photographs	Aerial photographs and remote sensing images based on the latitude and longitude of a location are available from: United States Geological Survey, EROS Data Center, Sioux Falls, South Dakota 57198 605/594-6151
Household hazards	FREE. Pamphlet: *Household Hazardous Waste: What You Should and Shouldn't Do.* Contact Water Pollution Control Federation, 601 Wythe Street, Alexandria, VA 22314. Send a self-addressed stamped envelope.
Natural hazards	FREE. Set of eight posters illustrating volcanic eruptions, earthquakes, landslides, mudflows, and flooding. Write to U.S. Geological Survey, 119K National Center, Reston, VA 22092

Read More About It

Brady, N. C. *The Nature and Property of Soils.* 8th ed. New York: Macmillan, 1974.

Judson, S., and M. E. Kauffman. *Physical Geology.* Englewood Cliffs, NJ: Prentice-Hall, 1990.

U.S. Department of Agriculture, Soil Conservation Service. *What Is a Watershed?* (Pamphlet PA-420). Washington, DC: U.S. Government Printing Office, 1969.

Weller, M. *Freshwater Marshes—Ecology and Wildlife Management.* Minneapolis: University of Minnesota Press, 1981.

Wolbarst, A., ed. *Environment in Peril.* Washington, DC: Smithsonian Press, 1991.

6

THE AIR WE ALL BREATHE!

Take a deep breath! About 99 percent of the volume of air you inhaled is gaseous nitrogen and oxygen. You also inhaled traces of other gases, minute droplets of various liquids, and tiny particles of various solids. The atmosphere is the crucible for all these materials; it is the delicate envelope that surrounds our living world. In this chapter you will investigate how natural and human-made changes combine to affect climate, distribution of life forms, protection against radiation, and the exchange and renewal of life-sustaining gases.

GASES AND PARTICLES

Air pollutants are either gases or particles, from molecules, such as carbon dioxide, nitrogen oxides, sulfur oxides, to larger organic compounds. Air contaminants affect the health of individuals, plants, animals, fabrics, building materials, and other natural resources.

• Go to the library and identify the major sources of gaseous and particulate pollution. How are these emissions generated as well as controlled?

• Investigate particulate emissions by first locating smoke-stacks on a map. Determine the direction of the prevailing winds and mark it on the map. Visit some of the sites and sample the air at known distances both downwind and upwind of the stacks as follows.

What you need:

stiff white cards, 4-in square
clear plastic wrap
petroleum jelly
sticky tape
thumbtacks
magnifying glass
   or dissecting microscope

What to do:

1. Number the cards and cover each one with clear plastic wrap. Be sure the wrap is drawn tightly over the card and secured in the back with sticky tape.

2. Coat the plastic wrap with a *thin film* of petroleum jelly.

3. Tack the cards outside on dry days at various locations, both upwind and downwind of smokestacks or other industrial emis-sion sources. In your notebook, record card number, location, and the wind direction and speed there.

4. Retrieve the cards after set periods of between 2 and 12 hours and record this exposure time. Examine them with a magni-fying glass or under a dissecting microscope.
— With pieces of a clean cloth, rub needles of evergreens near your sampling points to pick up any accumulated pollutants, and study with a magnifying glass. Sample trees near road-ways.

Analyzing your data:

- Use Figure 6-1 as a guide in identifying particulates. To aid in identification, you may want to take samples of emissions from known sources—bus and automobile exhausts, pollen from nearby flower beds—soils carried away by the wind during spring plowing, and so on to compile a "reference library" of emission and contaminate materials.
- Can you see patterns in the way emission contaminants are scattered by the wind? Do contaminants decrease after a heavy or light rain?
- If you live near a large urban area, see whether your findings correlate with "pollution indices" printed in the newspaper. The pollution index is a measure of the amount of suspended particulates in the air.

VOLCANIC WINTER

The winter of '83/'84 was abnormally cool, noted Benjamin Franklin—in *1784*. He speculated that the cause was a "haze" of material ejected from the volcanic eruption of Skaptar Jokull in Iceland. Abnormally cold temperatures and wet conditions have also followed other major volcanic eruptions; in some cases, the average temperature decreased as much as half a degree Celsius! Scientists today, as in yesteryear, attribute these climatic changes to the veil of volcanic debris—ash and aerosols— that can remain suspended for years, blocking direct sunlight but permitting heat to escape from the ground.

- There are strong indications that climatic change is upon us again, with the eruption of Mount Pinatubo in the spring of 1991. Review local climate data for 1991-93 (You can either contact the National Weather Service office near you or research daily climate reports in newspapers for a major city near you or a number of cities in the United States.) Can you find a correlation between the eruption and a shift in temperature or rainfall?
- The eruption of Mount Tambora in Indonesia in 1815 has

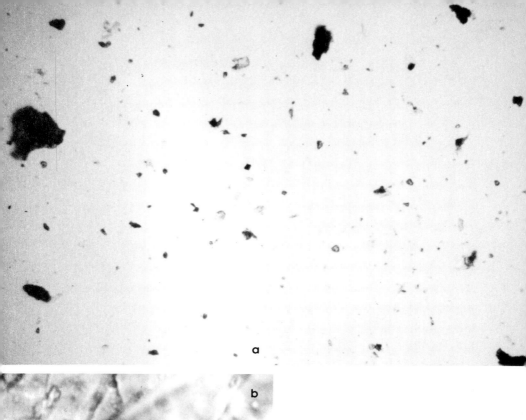

Figure 6-1
Visual Guide to Air Contaminants

(a) These are particulates—mostly carbon particles—from a city bus that burns diesel fuel. Diesel, a petroleum product, contains other impurities, such as sulfur, which is responsible for the plumes of black exhaust often coming from buses.

(b) This is a magnified view of an air filter that has had about 80 cubic feet of "fresh" country air passed through it. Can you find the tiny circular pollen grain?

the distinction of being the largest in human history. The eruption had a force exceeding that of 1 million atomic bombs and killed over 90,000 individuals! The following year, 1816, became known as "the year without a summer." Do some research to find out whether this characterization was truly deserved. If possible, try to verify similar consequences after the volcanic eruptions listed in the following table.

Mount Asama	Japan	1784
Mount Krakatoa	Indonesia	1883
Mount Katmai	Alaska	1912
Mount Etna	Sicily	1969
El Chichon	Mexico	1982
Nevado del Ruiz	Columbia	1985
Mount Pinatubo	Philippines	1991

SMOG VERSUS VOG

Vog—volcanic smog—is a mixture of volcanic ash, sulfur dioxide, and droplets of sulfurous acid. It forms when an eruption ejects large quantities of particulates and gases into the stratosphere 6 to 30 miles above the Earth. Its close relative, *smog*, is a combination of smoke and fog: that term was coined to describe London air quality conditions in the early part of the century. Both terms describe an optical effect—the scattering of light, by particulate matter. Let's investigate!

SUNSETS AND FOG LIGHTS
In rainbows, water droplets act as millions of tiny prisms, each refracting white light to form a spectrum of colors. In a prism, violet light bends the most because it has the shortest wavelength and red bends the least because it has the longest. Thus, the colors from a prism and in a rainbow are arranged according to wavelength as follows:
Red **O**range **Y**ellow **G**reen **B**lue **I**ndigo **V**iolet
Think of the name *Roy G. Biv* to remember the order.

When light rays strike molecules or other tiny particles, the light is sent off in new directions: that is, the light rays *scatter.* This optical effect helps explain why clear skies are blue. Air molecules, because they are extremely small, scatter more blue light than other colors. As you leave the atmosphere, the sky turns black because there are no air molecules to scatter light from the sun. Investigate optical light scattering and air pollution by doing these projects:

• When the sun is near the horizon, it looks orange or red because other colors have been scattered before the light reaches us. Air particulates enhance the effect. View sunsets and sunrises on days when the air is heavy with moisture versus clear, dry days. Do you notice any change in the quality of the sunset or sunrise?

• Correlate sunset color and brilliance with air quality reports and pollution indices in your local newspaper.

• Use your knowledge of light scattering to design a superior fog lamp. Put color acetate sheets over flashlight lenses and determine which color can be best seen—that is, which scatters the least amount of light—in fog. Compare your results to auto fog lamps; are the colors close? Why are high-beam lights not practical in heavy fog?

• Investigate reports of blue- and green-colored suns, which were common occurrences in nineteenth-century England and which still occur during dust storms in the deserts of Mongolia. Have such optical effects been reported after any recent volcanic eruptions? Could you design an experiment to duplicate this optical effect?

VISUALIZING VOLCANIC SUNSETS AND GLOWSETS
It is estimated that Mount Pinatubo spewed almost as much sulfur dioxide (SO_2) into the air as United States industry emits in a year—approximately 20 million tons! In the stratosphere, SO_2 combines with water to form sulfurous acid (H_2SO_3.) Initial estimates place the ash cloud of Mount Pinatubo some 15 miles above the Earth.

Stratospheric volcanic aerosol clouds make for spectacular sunsets. The thicker the cloud, the brighter and longer the sunset display. Sunsets may be enhanced by volcanic clouds as long as three years after an eruption. Most "normal" sunsets come from water vapor and other suspended particulates in the troposphere, which is below the stratosphere.

A *glowset* is the afterglow on the horizon after the sun has set. The higher the volcanic aerosol cloud is in the stratosphere, the longer its glowset.

• Watch sunsets and glowsets from a point with a clear view of the horizon. Check your local paper for the exact time of sunset and then keep careful watch at that time on the western horizon. You should see evidence of Mount Pinatubo's aerosol cloud approximately 10 to 15 minutes *after* sunset. It usually lasts another 10 to 15 minutes depending upon the cloud's thickness and atmospheric conditions. Sunrises are equally spectacular. Plan to view the eastern horizon at least 30 minutes *before* the sunrise. Photograph your observations with a 35 mm camera. Try an f/16 setting and low-speed film (ASA 64).

For advanced young scientists

UNDERSTANDING THE GREENHOUSE EFFECT

The *greenhouse effect* is the rise in global temperature caused by an accumulation of gases in the atmosphere that "trap" the sun's heat and prevent it from dissipating back into space. In this project you will build a model demonstrating the greenhouse effect.

What you need:

lamp with a squeeze clamp having a 200-watt incandescent
    bulb, mounted on a stand
clear plastic pop bottle (2 liter); cut as shown in Figure 6-2
digital thermometer, calibrated in degrees Celsius (°C)
clear plastic film

dark soil (8 ounces)
alkalizing tablets
wooden dowel (¼-inch diameter; 15 inches long)
plastic wrap (6 inches square)
small, shallow dish that can easily fit into pop bottle
watch with second hand, graph paper, colored pencils,
    rubber band

What to do:

Part One—Air Heating and Cooling

1. Place about 8 ounces of dark soil in the bottom of the cut plastic pop bottle.

2. Suspend the digital thermometer with string or wire to the halfway mark inside the bottle.

3. Cover the opening in the bottle with plastic film held in place with a rubber band.

4. Position the pop bottle under the lamp, about 5-6 inches away.

5. Allow the thermometer to come to room temperature. Record the starting temperature.

6. Turn on the lamp and record temperatures at 1-minute intervals for 20 minutes.

7. Turn off the lamp; record temperatures at 1-minute intervals for 20 minutes.

Part Two—CO_2 Heating and Cooling:

1. Remove the plastic film and thermometer from the bottle. Use the wooden dowel to tamp a depression in the topsoil.

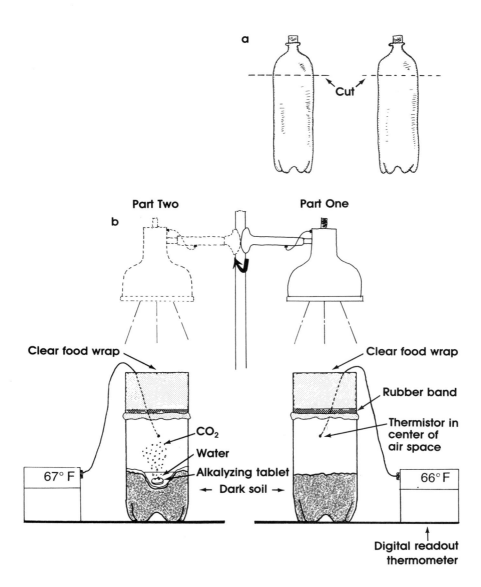

a

Cut

Part Two

b

Part One

Clear food wrap

Clear food wrap

Rubber band

Thermistor in center of air space

CO_2

Water

Alkalyzing tablet

← Dark soil →

67° F

66° F

Digital readout thermometer

Figure 6-2   Understanding the Greenhouse Effect
Simulate the greenhouse effect in a pop bottle. Compare the temperatures in a pop bottle with normal air to those in a pop bottle in which carbon dioxide gas is generated by an alkalyzing tablet.

Carefully press a 6-inch square of plastic wrap into the depression and fill it with approximately 1 ounce of water. Add 10 alkalizing tablets one at a time to generate CO_2.

2. Repeat Steps 2 to 7 of Part One.

Analyzing your data:
- Graph the heating and cooling cycles for both CO_2 and air.
    — Was the increase in temperature greater in air or the CO_2 environment?
    — Which environment lost more heat upon cooling?
    — Which environment showed the greater temperature gain at the conclusion of the experiment?
    — Does this project accurately model the greenhouse effect, or does it focus on the ability of CO_2 to absorb heat energy?
- What is the function of the dark soil in this experiment? Design an experiment that investigates the effect of different surfaces, including water in large lakes, on heat absorption and atmospheric temperatures.

RADON

Radon-222 is a colorless, odorless, tasteless gas produced by the radioactive decay of uranium-238. Small amounts of U-238 are found in most soil and rock, but this isotope is much more concentrated in underground deposits of uranium, phosphate, granite, and shale rock.

When radon gas from such deposits percolates upward through rock fissures and soil, it quickly dissipates to the atmosphere and decays to harmless levels. If it is trapped or accumulates in basements, it can build up to high levels that can greatly affect the health of occupants.

- Research this topic at the library to create a poster that illustrates how radon gas can accumulate in homes as well as how it can be reduced (see Learn More About It).

• If you live in a detached house, mobile home, or first three floors of an apartment building, suggest to an adult that radon levels should be measured, as the surgeon general recommends. Use only an approved EPA radon detection kit, available in hardware stores or through mail-order catalogs.

NATURE'S AIR QUALITY MONITORS—LICHENS

Lichens are a curious association of alga and fungus. Observe this biological commingling firsthand by collecting a lichen, cutting through its body, and observing it through either a magnifying glass or a dissecting microscope. Use Figure 6-3 as a guide to lichen identification and anatomy.

Lichens are extremely sensitive to air pollution, especially to sulfur dioxide. This sensitivity is often obvious in urban areas where trees face city traffic; here, lichens grow only on the side of the tree opposite traffic flow!

• The following technique will help you quantify lichen distribution and gauge their effectiveness as bioindicators of local air quality. When lichen hunting, look for walnut, ash, maple, and ginkgo trees; these are excellent lichen substrates!

Trunk transect method: With thumbtacks, secure a cloth tape measure around a tree at chest height, with the "zero" mark facing west. Place colored thumbtacks at the other compass points (north, east, and south). Begin counting lichen species at the west compass point, continuing clockwise to north, then east and south: record the species that touch the top of the tape measure at regular increments, such as every 2 inches. Conduct transects on at least five trees within a given study area. Compute averages for each study area.

— If feasible, try conducting transects within urban, suburban, and outlying countryside settings. Conduct transect surveys that address some of these questions: Are lichen populations affected in overall numbers or in diversity by environmental influences such as light, wind direction, or proximity to industrial activity? For example, do your transect

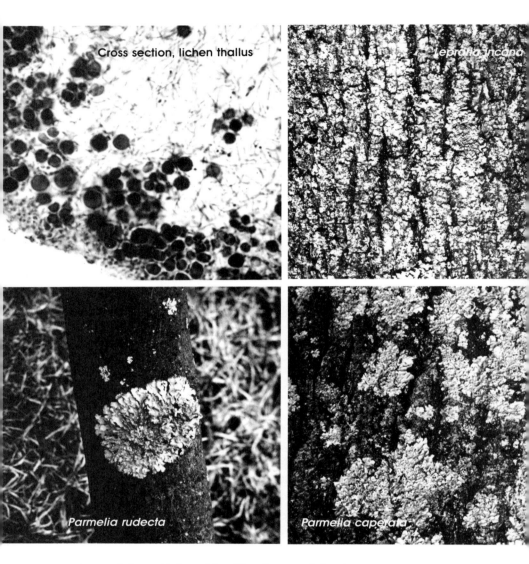

Cross section, lichen thallus

Lepraria incana

Parmelia rudecta

Parmelia caperata

Figure 6-3   Lichen Identification and Anatomy
These are some common lichen forms. The first is a
photomicrograph of the cross section of a lichen thallus—the
body of the lichen. The other photographs show different
types of lichens as you would see them on trees.

counts show lichen growing in only one compass direction, such that it is shielded against prevailing winds?

• Can you find evidence of lichens, such as *Lepraria,* that are pollutant-tolerant? Other organisms, such as the protist *Trentepolia,* whose crustlike yellow growth is often visible on moist stones, bark, and leaves, is another indicator of polluted air.

— To illustrate your findings, make color overlays for a map of the area you surveyed. For example, use different colors to represent lichen types occurring within a geographic area.

USING OZONE DETECTORS

Ozone (O_3) is a form of oxygen that collects in the upper atmosphere, specifically in the stratosphere 14 to 19 miles above the earth. It protects living things by shielding 95 to 99 percent of the sun's harmful ultraviolet (UV) rays from the earth. Ozone forms when UV radiation strikes ordinary oxygen (O_2); lightning also converts some oxygen to ozone. Industrial chemicals called chlorofluorocarbons (CFCs) may destroy this ozone layer.

Most ozone in the lower atmosphere is considered an air pollutant. It comes from chemical reactions between sunlight and pollutants already in the atmosphere.

• Use your nose as an ozone detector! Go outside immediately after a thunderstorm and see whether you can detect the pungent smell of ozone.

• Ozone degrades natural rubber. Obtain some rubber from natural latex rubber gloves available in pharmacy or medical supply stores. Remove the bottom (usually black) plastic support from a pop bottle by soaking it in hot water. Cut out a piece of latex rubber from the palm area of a glove, stretch it over the opening of the support, and secure it. Make a number of these ozone test membranes. Place the membranes in various locations—urban, suburban, and rural—and monitor the condition of the membrane using a magnifying glass for a period of 4 to 6 weeks. Record your findings in your field notebook. Which environmental condition produces the greatest deterioration of rubber? Is it due to ozone alone?

VANISHING PELLETS!

Currently the United States uses about 200 million cubic feet per year of polystyrene loose-fill, the round or peanut-shaped pellets you find in packages mailed to you. CFCs are used in the manufacture of the pellets to make them expand, or puff up. And although some companies try to reuse the loose-fill, most of it is disposed of in a landfill.

To reduce CFC use and to save landfill space, a new type of loose-fill packaging material consisting of 95 percent cornstarch and 5 percent polyvinyl alcohol has been developed. This material contributes to pollution reduction in a unique way: it disappears! Well, not exactly—the material is degraded by water into components that bacteria break down further to carbon dioxide!

Obtain some of this packing material that looks like short puffy open cylinders, or write to request a sample and additional information to American Excelsior Company, 850 Ave. H East, P.O. Box 5067, Arlington, TX 76005-5067, 817/640-1555.

• Weigh 100 grams of this material on a scale. Place the material in a bucket and add a quart of water. Record what happens in your field notebook. Water test plants such as lawn grass, bean plants, or tomato plants with this solution and control plants with distilled water. Are there any potential harmful effects should liquid from landfill containing the material leach to groundwater?

• Test other concentrations of the solution; dissolve larger quantities of the packing material in the same volume of water. Is this material a truly environmentally safe product?

STUDYING ELECTROMAGNETIC RADIATION

There is increasing concern over health effects from prolonged exposures to electromagnetic radiation (EMR).

Radiation is the invisible waves of electrical and magnetic energy that come from appliances, power lines, computers, and other electrical devices. It comes in many different wavelengths, such as radio waves, microwaves, infrared rays, visible light, ultraviolet light, X rays, and gamma rays. But concern recently has focused on the longer wavelengths that power homes; these waves oscillate 60 times a second or 60 Hertz.

In 1820, the Danish scientist Hans Oersted discovered that a conductor carrying an electrical current is surrounded by a magnetic field. When he placed a magnetized needle from a compass near a wire where current flowed, the needle deflected. The strength of a magnetic field is measured in units of *gauss*. The earth's magnetic field is relatively weak, measuring only ½ gauss; in contrast, the magnetic field of a cyclotron, a particle accelerator, has a field strength of over 20,000 gauss!

Today, technicians use sophisticated devices—gaussmeters—to measure the electromagnetic fields emanating from power lines and other electromagnetic devices. In many states, there are regulations governing how strong such electromagnetic fields are. You can use a compass as a crude, but very inexpensive, gaussmeter and study electromagnetic radiation by doing the following project:

MEASURING ELECTROMAGNETIC FIELDS
What you need:

magnetic compass
length of bell wire (approximately 10 feet)
various battery types (alkaline versus dry-cell lantern battery) at
    different voltages (1.5– 12-volt—no higher!)
ruler (12 inches)
tape, electrical
wire strippers

What to do:

1.   Create a coil of wire with an inner diameter of approximately 4 inches; make sure to leave a 24-inch free-length of wire at both ends. Use electrical tape to maintain the coil.

2.   Bend the free ends of wire upward. Strip approximately ½ inch of insulation from both ends. Use electrical tape to affix each wire to a pole of a battery.

3. Tape the ruler to a background support, such as a wall or pile of books. Place a magnetic compass directly in front of the ruler with "N" facing north.

4. Begin by using a 1.5-volt cell to power your magnetic induction coil. Carefully lower the coil, oriented horizontally toward the compass. Note the height above the compass at which the needle deflects. Record the height and the direction of deflection in number of degrees in your field notebook. Continue lowering the coil until it rests around the compass itself. Observe and record any other changes. Change the polarity of the electrical field by reversing the wires at the battery's terminals and repeat the experiment. Does the compass needle change direction? Can you explain why? Does the force of the field depend on distance from the coil?

— Try this experiment with different battery voltages. Is field strength affected by voltage? Hypothesize what would happen if you fashioned a coil out of an extension cord plugged into an outlet and placed it around a magnetic compass. HINT: Household current is 120 volts and it is alternating current (AC), which means it oscillates at (60 H), as opposed to the constant direct current (DC) of batteries.

ADDITIONAL ELECTROMAGNETIC
RADIATION PROJECTS
• Use your magnetic compass "gaussmeter" to detect and measure electromagnetic fields from energized household appliances. In your field notebook record the degrees of needle deflection and the direction as well as distance of the compass from the appliance when deflection first occurs. Begin by investigating these sources: television set, electric blanket, fluorescent versus incandescent lights, garage doors, remote-control devices, toaster, microcomputer, hair dryer. Compare readings

taken at set distance—6 inches, for example—increments from each device.

• Investigate outdoor sources: at the base of electric poles having a step-down transformer, underneath power lines running from a utility pole to your house, at a utility company meter where electrical service enters your house, underneath the path of high-voltage power lines. Compare and contrast readings taken at 10- 25- and 50-foot increments away from these energized sources. Are the compass deflections any different from those inside your home?

HOW SOME ORGANISMS RESPOND
TO ELECTRICAL FIELDS

Galvanotaxis describes how an organism moves in response to an electrical potential gradient. You can study how certain microlife forms, such as the ciliate *Paramecium*, respond to increasing voltage currents by doing the following:

What you need:

microscope slide (1 by 3 inches)
epoxy
bell wire (12 inches)
lantern battery (6-volt)
insulation stripper
medicine dropper
Paramecium (from a pond or a biological supply house)
black construction paper (4 inch square)
sandpaper
stereo (dissecting) microscope

What to do:

1. Follow Figure 6-4 to construct an electrical cell on a microscope slide. (Polish the copper electrodes with sandpaper to assure electron transfer to the water.)

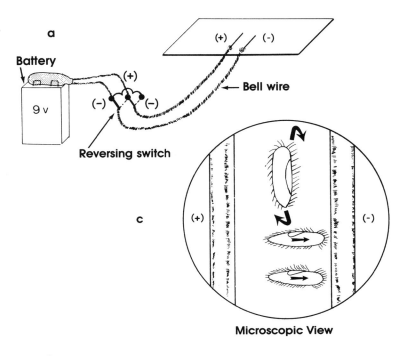

a

Battery

9 v

(+)

(−) (−)

Reversing switch

(+) (−)

Bell wire

c

(+) (−)

Microscopic View

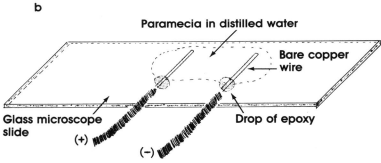

b

Paramecia in distilled water

Bare copper wire

Glass microscope slide

Drop of epoxy

(+)

(−)

Figure 6-4   Investigating Galvanotaxis

You can observe how paramecium and other microlife forms
respond to electric fields with this setup. Close the contact
between the battery and the slide to energize the specimen
and watch what happens under the microscope.

2. Place the slide on the stage of a dissecting microscope. If a microscope is not available, place the slide on top of a piece of black construction paper and view with a magnifying glass.

3. Flood the area between the two electrodes with drops of paramecium culture or pond water containing paramecia. Make sure there is good contact between the water and the electrodes.

4. Energize the slide by connecting the wires leading from the slide to the poles of the lantern dry cell. Note the location of (+) and (−) poles.

— Observe and determine at which pole paramecia congregate. Cells that congregate near the (−) pole are termed *negatively galvanotropic*; attraction to the (+) pole means the cell(s) are positively galvanotropic. Record your observations in your field notebook. If possible, observe individual cells under a stereomicroscope to determine how the electrical field affects cells.
— Experiment by applying additional current. Connect dry cells in series:

$$(+) \rightarrow (-) / (-) \rightarrow (+).$$

— What happens if a cell touches the wire electrode?
— Experiment with other microlife forms to determine whether other cells are affected by electrical fields.

Learn More About It

RADON   *The Geology of Radon.* For sale by the U.S. Government Printing Office, Superintendent of Documents, Mail Stop SSOP, Washington, DC 20402-9328. ISBN 0-16-037974-1.
Radon Reduction in New Construction can be obtained FREE from state radon-protection offices or the National Association of Homebuilders,

Attention: William Young, 15th and M Streets NW, Washington, DC 20005.

Radon Reduction Methods can be obtained FREE from the Environmental Protection Agency, 401 M Street SW, Washington, DC 20460

Read More About It

Becker, R. O. *Cross Currents: The Promise of Electromedicine, the Perils of Electropollution.* New York: St. Martin's, 1990.

"How Accurate Are Radon Detectors?" *Consumer's Report.* 74:4 (April 1, 1991), 15.

Brodeur, Paul. "Annals of Radiation—The Cancer at Slater School." *The New Yorker.* 68:42 (December 7, 1992), 86.

The Great Powerline Coverup: How Utilities and the Government Are Trying to Hide the Cancer Hazard Posed by Electromagnetic Fields. Boston: Little, Brown, 1993.

Brown, M. *The Toxic Cloud.* New York: Harper & Row, 1987.

Courrier, K., and J. MacKenzie. *The Greenhouse Trap.* Boston: Beacon Press, 1990.

Environmental Protection Agency. *The Inside Story: A Guide to Indoor Air Quality.* USEPA-88-114. Washington, DC: Environmental Protection Agency, 1988.

———*The Potential Effects of Global Climate Change on the United States.* USEPA-88-026. Washington, DC: Environmental Protection Agency, 1988.

———*Radon Reduction Methods: A Homeowner's Guide.* USEPA-86-005. Environmental Protection Agency, 1986.

Fisher, David E. *Fire and Ice: The Greenhouse Effect, Ozone Depletion and Nuclear Winter.* New York: Harper & Row, 1990.

Fisher, Marshall. *The Ozone Layer.* New York: Chelsea House, 1992.

Gay, K. *Ozone.* New York: Watts, 1989.

Hale, Mason. *How to Know the Lichens.* Dubuque, IA: Wm. C. Brown, 1979.

Johnson, Rebecca. *Investigating the Ozone Hole.* Minneapolis: Lerner Publications, 1993.

Lyman, Francesca, with Irving Mintzer, Kathleen Courrier, and James MacKenzie. The *Greenhouse Trap: What We're Doing to the Atmosphere and How We Can Stop Global Warming.* Boston: Beacon Press, 1990.

Maduro, Rogelio. *The Holes in the Ozone Scare: The Scientific Evidence That the Sky Isn't Falling.* Washington, D.C.: 21st Century Science Associates, 1992.

National Academy of Sciences. *Air Pollution, the Automobile, and Human Health.* Washington, DC: National Academy Press, 1988.

Office of Technology Assessment. *Catching Our Breath: Next Steps for Reducing Urban Ozone.* Washington, DC: U.S. Government Printing Office, 1989.

Phillips, Ed. *In the Atmosphere: The Greenhouse Factor.* Phoenix, Ariz.: D.B. Clark, 1990.

"Radon Detectors: How to Find Out If Your House Has a Radon Problem." *Consumer Reports.* July 1987.

Rainis, Kenneth. *Nature Projects for Young Scientists.* New York: Watts, 1989.

Roan, Sharon. *Ozone Crisis: The 15-Year Evolution of a Sudden Global Emergency.* New York: Wiley, 1989.

Shea, Cynthia Pollack. "Protecting the Ozone Layer." In *State of the World 1989,* by Lester Brown et al. New York: W. W. Norton & Co., 1989.

Young, L. *Sowing the Wind: Reflections on the Earth's Atmosphere.* Englewood Cliffs, NJ: Prentice-Hall, 1990.

7

TEN PROJECTS TO
HELP THE ENVIRONMENT

The following projects—along with related ones in the preceding chapters—will help make you more aware of exactly how we impact the environment.

PROJECT 1

Conducting a Home Environmental Audit

An *audit* is a systematic inspection that should uncover anything requiring change. Audit your home for the following items (feel free to add some of your own) and see how you and your household measure up environmentally!

[ ] Lights are shut off when not in use; fluorescent lighting in place of incandescent lighting.

[ ] Water-saving devices in shower and toilet.

[ ] Energy-efficient heating systems in fireplace, furnace, or heat pump.

[ ] Energy-efficient appliances.

[ ] No chemical herbicides/pesticides or inorganic fertilizers.

[ ] Grass clippings, leaves, branches, and so on, composted.

[ ]   Walls Insulated at least to R-19.
[ ]   Recycling of plastics, metals, paper, and other
        materials.
[ ]   Energy-efficient windows.
[ ]   Car pooling to work.
[ ]   Cotton fiber instead of synthetic fiber.
[ ]   Shade trees and shrubs planted near house.
[ ]   Use of household chemicals (detergents, cleaners, etc.)
        evaluated. See Project 10.

PROJECT 2

Establishing A Nature Trail
One of the first self-guided nature trails was created in Bear
Mountain State Park, Harriman, New York, over fifty years ago.
The public was guided on a path to areas with signs describing
the ecology and unique local geologic and ecologic conditions,
along with exhibits on the diversity and uniqueness of local wild-
life. (See Figure 7-1.) For most of the viewers, residents of New
York City, this was their introduction to nature's landscape.

Creating a nature trail is rewarding and will serve to sharpen
your powers of observation and increase your awareness of our
natural world. It is also hard work! Begin by obtaining permission
from a landowner; abide by whatever conditions he or she sets
forth for the use of the property. You must work under adult
supervision; enlist the aid of a science teacher or other adult
who is knowledgeable in the natural sciences.

• Begin by deciding what the objective of the trail is. Will
it identify area vegetation or point out unique environmental
features? Stake out the trail with stakes or colored buttons fas-
tened to trees.

• Obtain field guides and other reference works (see the
end of this chapter) to identify plants along the trail.

• Create signs that identify life forms and unique natural
geologic or ecologic conditions or that just point the way.

• Consider creating special dioramas, models, relief (topographic) maps, or displays that further explain and illustrate various natural aspects of your selected locality. For example, you

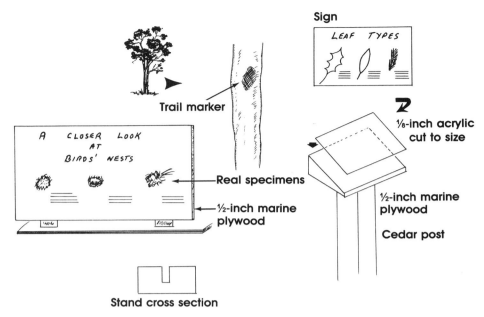

Sign

Trail marker

Real specimens

½-inch marine plywood

⅛-inch acrylic cut to size

½-inch marine plywood

Cedar post

Stand cross section

Figure 7-1   Trailside Nature Signs

Create your own trailside nature signs to highlight important environmental conditions along your nature trail. In the photograph, Caroline Rainis is getting trailside information at the Cummings Nature Center in Naples, New York.

may want to create a display of deciduous leaf types, as well as bark and winter twig samples, from trees along the trail, or of birds' nests or pinecones. These displays might be housed in a special area set up on "open trail" days—days when you and your friends conduct special tours.

• Consider giving a special video tour; have a friend film you narrating a tour along the trail.

PROJECT 3

Marketing a Wetland

Wetlands—swamps, salt- and freshwater marshes, bogs, detention ponds, ditches, and vernal pools (mudholes that fill in springtime)—are areas that are saturated or covered by water at least part of the year. They contain specific types of plants and have hydric soils (wet, dense soils that usually have little or no oxygen). They can form where water collects in depressions in the land or where soil and organic matter collect in ponds or other water bodies.

Many scientists believe that wetlands are the "marrow of nature"—the most important natural ecosystems on Earth—because they support an incredible diversity of life-forms and perform myriad functions essential for maintaining the web of life. They serve as buffers against flood damage, they purify water by reducing nitrogen and phosphorus levels, and they provide habitats for plants and animals alike.

• Identify a wetland near where you live. Get permission to explore and study it. Conduct surveys to determine its physical and biological makeup.

— Create a display that informs local residents about the wetland and its benefits for a bank or library or for your town hall.

— Conduct a diversity study (see chapter 2) of life forms living in microhabitats of the wetland such as muds, grasses, and shore area. Do wetland habitats have higher diversity indices than terrestrial or pond habitats?

— Use your camera and video camera to record life forms and landscape features that illustrate why wetlands are important.

• Study wetland plants; try to find out why they thrive in flooded conditions. Study their root and leaf structures with a magnifying glass. What special internal structural characteristics do the flat leaves of cattails have? Try cutting a leaf in half and examining with a magnifying glass.

• If possible, visit marshes in coastal areas. See whether you can design a project that shows how smooth cordgrasses minimize the impact of waves in shore areas.

• Make casts of leaf surfaces to find out where the greatest concentration of stomates—the tiny openings through which gases pass—is located: above or under the water.

— Make stomate impressions by painting a leaf surface with a thin layer of Duco® cement. Allow to dry. Carefully separate the dried layer of cement from the leaf with fine-point tweezers. Dip the cement cast into water and lay it on a clean microscope slide. Observe it under low-power magnification in a compound microscope.

• A good way to get acquainted with wetland microlife is to set up a wetland aquarium that simulates your study area.

PROJECT 4

Create a Mini Wildlife Refuge

Work with your friends to reestablish habitats for wildlife. Make sure you have adult permission to conduct your project. First conduct a survey of animal and plant life in and around the area in which you will be working. Make a list of habitat improvements you want to make. Use the following list as a guide:

Build nesting/roosting boxes for birds, bats, and insects.
Plant trees that provide food and cover for birds, fowl, and
    other wildlife.
Construct watering holes 1½ to 3 inches in depth.
Construct brush piles that provide additional cover.

- Contact your state Conservation Department, Department of Agriculture office, or local nature center to learn what types of plants and ground cover are appropriate for your area.
- Consult the reference sources at the end of this chapter for plans for constructing nesting boxes. Get your plans approved by a conservation officer or by your science teacher.
- Enlist the aid of your friends to construct the habitat. Once your habitat improvements are complete, keep a log in your field notebook of which animal and plant forms move in and exploit it.
- Try to get your habitat certified by the National Wildlife Federation's Backyard Wildlife Habitat Program. Write to National Wildlife Federation, 1400 16th Street NW, Washington, DC 20036-2266.

PROJECT 5

Monitoring Waterways for Polluters
Thousands of young people all over the world are involved in water quality–monitoring projects such as Global Rivers Environmental Education Network (GREEN) or Watershed Worlds. GREEN links schools all over the world in Asia, Africa, Europe, North and South America through newsletters, workshops, and computer conferencing. See Learn More About It for additional information.

PROJECT 6

Cool Shade!
Conduct the following projects to gather evidence that trees are climatic moderators; once you are convinced, encourage tree planting around buildings.
- It is not uncommon for wooded areas to be 10° cooler than surrounding areas. Take temperature measurements near where you live to determine the cooling conditions offered by wooded growth areas.
- Place thermometers around two buildings—one shaded by trees and the other not shaded. Be sure that the relative

positions of thermometers are the same on both buildings; height above ground, orientation to north, and so on, should be similar. Compare temperature measurements.

PROJECT 7

Exploring the Three
R's—Reduction, Reuse, and Recycling

The prescription for the twenty-first century is the 3 R's—*reduce reuse*, and *recycle*. Here are some projects that explore aspects of each of them:

Reduce the Amount of Waste Produced

- *Napkin saved is a volume returned*—Calculate how much landfill space would be saved if your household switched from paper napkins and towels to cloth napkins.
- *Chlorine and you*—Chlorine is an extremely reactive element. When released to the environment it can form toxic compounds like chloroform and dioxin. Investigate hydrogen peroxide as a substitute for liquid chlorine bleach in cleaning fabrics.

Caution: **Wear protective gloves and eyewear when working with chemical solutions. Do this investigation under adult supervision.**

— Obtain chlorine bleach and a 3 percent hydrogen peroxide solution from a local grocery store or supermarket.

Place equal amounts (1 to 3 ounces) of each cleaner in separate plastic containers. *Caution:* **Never mix chlorine bleach with hydrogen peroxide solution.** Soil a handkerchief or piece of cotton cloth; create a combination of grass, soil, and jelly stains or other stain of your choosing. Cut this piece into two equal parts and place each in a cleaning solution for approximately 1 hour. Remove and rinse each piece under running water. Are the cleaning solutions similar in effectiveness?

— Go to the library and research how chlorinated compounds can affect water and air quality.

• *No deposit/no return*—Used motor oil is an environmental hazard when disposed of improperly. Many local auto repair shops burn used motor oil rather than natural gas for heating. Visit such an establishment and prepare a report that documents how much used motor oil is burned, how much heat energy is generated, and what the estimated cost savings are.

• *Hitting the road*—reuse projects are as creative as the materials they seek to recycle. The nations' highways are fast becoming a favorite target for the "beneficial reuse" of waste materials such as scrap tires, glass, petroleum-contaminated soils, and scrap roofing. They are being used as roadbed aggregate! Contact your State Conservation Department to find out whether it administers BUD applications—"Beneficial Reuse Determinations" and has a Materials Reuse Division. Find out what types of materials and which companies are certified for reuse in your state.

Recycle Waste Materials

• *Leftovers*—In many instances mechanics and homeowners do not adequately drain *all* the motor oil from containers when changing engine oil or when accepting used motor oil for recycling. Often a considerable amount is still left in the container—and usually finds its way to a landfill.

Caution: Be sure to wear protective gloves and eyewear; work under adult supervision.

With adult permission, collect discarded motor oil containers from garages and lawn mower repair shops. Take them home and measure how much oil remains in each container. Keep records of your findings. On a map draw a circle around the area where you collected the containers. This will represent a motor oil "unit." Calculate how many such units are present in an area that you know sends its solid waste to a landfill. Estimate how much motor oil is being discarded and may be landfilled.

PROJECT 8

How Does Your Grass Grow?
Every year the average household applies 50 to 100 pounds of fertilizers/herbicides to the acre in search of the perfect, unblemished lawn. With landowner permission, over the course of a typical season, compare plots that use different lawn care practices: Create two marked plots, each at least 20-foot square. On plot 1 apply commercial fertilizer/herbicide as recommended by the manufacturer; cut the grass at the usual height. On plot 2, cut to 3 inches and allow the clippings to be spread evenly over the cut area. Do not water either plot; keep track of how much rain falls with a rain gauge. At the end of the season compare: number of weeds in each plot; length of "green time" in days; cost of applying commercial herbicide/fertilizer.

PROJECT 9

Improve Energy Efficiency
The most important thing you can do to reduce air pollution and ozone depletion, slow projected global climate change, and help your household save money is to improve energy efficiency. Compile action lists that you and the members of your household can follow. Include the topic areas in the following table.

Activity	Percentage
Transportation	Consumes 50 percent
Home heating	Consumes 25 percent
Cooking, refrigeration, and appliance usage	Consumes 9 percent
Lighting, cooling, and air-conditioning	Consumes 7 percent

Source: Environmental Protection Agency.

- Calculate your household "carbon bubble"—the amount of carbon released into the atmosphere every year due to energy consumption. (Use the values presented in carbon cycle projects in Chapter 3.)

PROJECT 10

Evaluating Alternatives
to Common Household Chemicals

Compare commercial household chemical products to some of the alternatives listed in the table. Document the names of all the chemicals in the commercial product compared with the alternative formulae. Go to the library to research why the chemicals are used in commercial products. Are the alternatives environmentally safer? Record all your findings in your field notebook.

Caution: **Wear protective goggles, gloves, and apron.**

Product	Alternative*
Oven cleaner	Baking soda and water to make a paste; use scouring pad.
Toothpaste	Baking soda.
Window cleaner	Add 2 teaspoons white vinegar to 1 quart warm water.
Floor cleaner	Add ½ cup white vinegar to a bucket of hot water for tough spots; sprinkle borax and rub with sponge.
Mildew remover	Mix ½ cup white vinegar, ½ cup borax, and warm water.
Detergent	Washing soda (sodium carbonate monohydrate) or borax and soap powder.
Fabric softener	Add 1 cup white vinegar or ¼ cup baking soda to final rinse.

Learn More About It

POLLUTION
MONITORING

GREEN c/o School of Natural Resources, University of Michigan, Ann Arbor, MI 48109-1115. Phone: (313) 764-1410

WATERSHED WORLDS c/o Thames Science Center, Gallows Lane, New London, CT 06320. Phone: (203) 442-0391

ADOPT-A-STREAM FOUNDATION c/o Executive Director, Box 5558, Everett, WA 98201

RIVER WATCH NETWORK Executive Director, 153 State Street, Montpelier, VT 05602. This group can provide information and statistics on streams and rivers in your area.

WILDLIFE HABITAT

BAT CONSERVATION INTERNATIONAL has patterns for bat roosting boxes. Write to Bat Conservation International, P.O. Box 1622603, Austin, TX 78716

HOUSEHOLD HAZARDOUS
WASTE

WATER POLLUTION CONTROL FEDERATION: FREE pamphlet: *Household Hazardous Waste: What You Should and Shouldn't Do.* Water Pollution Federation, 601 Wythe Street, Alexandria, VA 22314. Send a self-addressed stamped envelope.

ANNOTATED LIST OF
EDUCATION MATERIALS

U.S. Environmental Protection
Agency Office of External Relations
and Education, Youth Programs
(A-108 EA), Room 823 W2, 401 M
Street SW, Washington, DC 20460

Read More About It

Berthold-Bond, Annie. *Clean and Green—The Complete Guide to Nontoxic and Environmentally Safe Housekeeping.* New York: Ceres Press, 1990.

Brown, Vinson. *The Amateur Naturalist's Handbook.* Englewood Cliffs, NJ: Prentice-Hall, 1980.

Durrell, G. *A Practical Guide for the Amateur Naturalist.* New York: Knopf, 1986.

Earthworks Group. *50 Simple Things Kids Can Do to Save the Earth.* Berkeley, Calif.: Earthworks Press, 1989.

Elkington, John. *The Green Consumer.* New York: Penguin Books, 1990.

Gutnick, Martin J. *Experiments That Explore—Recycling.* Hillside, N.J.: Enslow, 1993.

Hunter, Linda Mason. *The Healthy House: An Attic-to-Basement Guide to Toxin-Free Living.* Emmaus, Pa.: Rodale Press, 1989.

Makower, Joel. *The Green Consumer Supermarket Guide.* New York: Penguin Books, 1991.

Mitchell, John G. "Our Disappearing Wetlands." *National Geographic* 182: 4 (October 1992), 3.

Rainis, Kenneth. *Nature Projects for Young Scientists.* New York: Franklin Watts, 1989.

Sax, Irving, and Lewis, Richard, eds. *Hawley's Condensed Chemical Dictionary,* 11th Ed. New York: Van Nostrand Reinhold, 1987.

APPENDIX

WHERE TO OBTAIN MATERIALS

Most supply companies will supply materials if an order is accompanied by a check. One company (Edmund) will provide a catalog if you call; ask to borrow your teacher's catalogs for information about order numbers and prices.

Carolina Biological Supply Company
2700 York Road
Burlington, NC 27215
800/547-1733

Connecticut Valley Biological Supply Company
82 Valley Road
South Hampton, MA 01073
413/527-4030

Discovery Scope, Inc.
P.O. Box 607
Green Valley, AZ 85622
800/398-5404
(Unique hand-held single-lens microscopes)

Edmund Scientific
101 E. Glouster Pike
Barrington, NJ 08008
609/573-6250
(Equipment and apparatus only)

Science Kit and Boreal Laboratories
777 East Park Drive
Tonawanda, NY 14150
800/828-7777

WARD'S Natural Science Establishment
5100 West Henrietta Road
P.O. Box 92912
Rochester, NY 14692
800/962-2660

INDEX

Abiotic factors, 14
Acidity, 81, 83–85, 87–88
Acid rain, 83–85
    pH, 84
Advertising, 64–66
Air, 121–141
    electromagnetic
        radiation, 134–139
    gases and particles,
        121–123
    greenhouse effect,
        127–130
    lichens, 131–133
    ozone detectors, 133
    radon, 130–131
    smog versus vog,
        125–127
    vanishing pellets, 134
    volcanic winter,
        123–125

Air contaminants, 124
Allelopathy, 40
Aluminum, 72–73
Aquatic organisms, 85–88
Aquatic plants, 92

Bacteria, culturing and
    staining, 27–30
Bats, 152
Batteries, 69–71
Bed load, 116
Berlese apparatus, 26
Biodiversity, 19–42
    biological controls,
        40–41
    microlife, 27–36
    pesticides, 37–40
    plants, 36–37
Biological controls, 40–41
Biological insecticide, 40

Biomes, 12–14
Biopesticides, 41
Bioremediation, 29
Biosphere, designing, 14–16
Biosphere II, 15
Biotic components, 14
Books
    air, 140–141
    biodiversity, 41–42
    environment, 17–18
    land, 120
    recycling, 73–74
    water, 102

Carbon cycle, 50, 52–54
Cirrus, 45, 46, 48
Climax vegetation, 12
Closed ecosystems, 14–16
Clouds, 44, 45, 46, 73
Community, 14
Composting, 54–57
Computer on-line help, 17
Concentration, 80
Condensation nuclei, 48
Consumer, 14, 15, 27
Consumer ratio, 15
Control group, 12
Contour interval, 104
Contour line, 103
Creeks, 75
Cumulus, 45, 46

Data, 12
Decomposer, 14, 27
Dendrochronology, 37, 38
Depth profile, 95
Dethatching, 29
Dilution, 80

Ditches, 91
Diversity. See Biodiversity
Drift, 37–39

Education materials, 153
Electromagnetic radiation,
    134–139
Erosion, 113–114
Evaporation, 44, 45

Fertilizers and water, 88–91
Fire ecology, 57
Fog lights, 125–126
Food chains, 14
Food web, 14, 27
Fungus, 29, 31–33
    key to types, 32–33

Galvanotaxis, 138
Garbage, 57–59
Garbologists, 117
Gases and particles,
    121–123
Global warming, 20
Glowsets, 126–127
Greenhouse effect, 127–130
Green Report II, The, 65
Ground cover, 112–113
Ground litter, 20
Groundwater, 44
Growth rings, 37

Habitats, 19
Hazardous waste, 152
Horizons, 110
Humidity chart, 22–23
Hydrologic cycle, 43
Hypothesis, 12

Infiltration, 44, 48, 111
Information
    air, 139–140
    biodiversity, 41
    environment, 17
    land, 119–120
    recycling, 72–73
    water, 101–102
Insecticides, 39–41

Kingdoms, 14

Lakes, 91
Land, 103–120
    erosion, 113–114
    ground cover, 112–113
    landfills, 117–119
    shape of, 103–105
    slope of, 105, 107–108
    soil, 110–112
    a stream's load,
        115–116
    watersheds, 108, 110
Landfills, 117–119
Leeuwenhoek, Antony van,
    33–34
Lichens, 131–133
Loam, 111

Man, as threat, 19
Maps, topographic,
    103–108
Marshes, 91
Method, 12
Microlife, 27–36, 97
Mill broke, 65
Mitton, Jeffrey, 36

Nitrogen cycle, 48–50, 51

Observation, 12
Ozone detectors, 133

Palmer, C. Mervin, 94
Palmer index, 94, 98
Paper, 59–64, 72
Paradox Lake, 88
Parent material, 110
Pasteur, Louis, 12
Percolation, 111–112
Pesticides, 37–40
pH level, 75, 81–83
Photovoltaic cells, 71–72
Plants, 36–37, 92
    and water runoff,
        99–100
Plastics, 66–69, 72
Pollution, 152
    indicators, 94, 96–99
    water, 80–81
Polystyrene pellets, 134
Ponds, 91
Precipitation, 44, 45, 48
Producer, 14, 15, 27
Projects, 142
    alternatives to
        household chemicals,
        151–153
    cool shade, 147–148
    create wildlife refuge,
        146–147
    establish a nature trail,
        143–145
    how does grass grow?,
        150

home environmental
audit, 142–143
improve energy
efficiency, 150–151
marketing a wetland,
145–146
monitor waterways, 147
reduction, reuse,
recycling, 148–149
Protists, 27, 34
Psychrometer, 21

Radiation, 134–139
Radon, 130–131, 139–140
Rain forests, 19–20
Recycling, 43–74
advertising, 64–66
batteries, 69–71
carbon cycle, 50, 52–54
composting, 54–57
fire ecology, 57
natural, 29
nitrogen cycle, 48–50, 51
paper, 59–64
photovoltaic cells,
71–72
plastics, 66–69
trash and garbage,
57–59
water cycle, 43–48
Refuse audit, 58–59
Relative humidity chart,
22–23
Road salting, 100–101

Safety rules, 16–17
Scavengers, 15

Secchi disk, 93
Serendipity, 12
Smog, 125–127
Soil, 110–112
Solid waste, 57–58
Species diversity, 19
Springs, 75
Steel, 72
Storm water runoff, 99–101
Stratus, 45, 46
Streams, 75, 79, 115–116
Subsoil, 110
Succession, 12
Sunsets, 125–127
Surface water runoff, 44, 48,
88–91

Topographic maps,
103–108
constructing, 104–105
Topsoil, 110
Transpiration, 43, 44, 45
Trash, 57–59
Tree growth, 37
Trophic level, 14

Vog, 125–127
Volcanic winter, 123–125

Water, 75–102
acidity, 81–83
acid rain, 83–85
fast waters, 75–80
fertilizers and, 88–91
Paradox Lake, 88
pollutants, 80–81
pollution, 94, 96–99

Water (*cont.*)
    quiet waters, 91–94
    runoff, 44, 48, 88–91,
      99–101
    storm water runoff,
      99–101

Water cycle, 43–48
Watersheds, 108, 119
Wentworth scale, 112
Wetlands, 101–102
Wildlife habitat, 101, 152
World's largest organism, 36